TEST OF
COURAGE

Compiled by Pat Edwards and Wendy Body

Acknowledgements

We are grateful to the following for permission to reproduce copyright material; J M Dent & Sons, Ltd for the story 'The Playground' in *The First Margaret Mahy Story Book* by Margaret Mahy; Faber & Faber Ltd for an extract from *Gowie Corby Plays Chicken* by Gene Kemp; the author's agent for an extract from *Julie of the Wolves* by Jean Craighead George (pub Harper & Row), copyright (c) 1972 by Jean Craighead George; Victor Gollancz Ltd for an extract from *The Great Gilly Hopkins* by Katherine Paterson, (c) Katherine Paterson 1979; the author's agent for an extract from *The Young Legionary* by Douglas Hill (pub Pan Books, 1982); Hodder & Stoughton (Australia) Pty Ltd for an extract from the story 'Undyarning' in *Young & Brave* by Mavis Thorpe Clark (pub 1984); Macmillan Publishing Co for the poem 'Daniel' in *Collected Poems* by Vachel Lindsay (pub Macmillan, New York, 1925); Methuen Children's Books Ltd for the story 'Quaka Raja' in *Listen to this Story* by Grace Hallworth; Sidgwick & Jackson Ltd for an extract from *Islands in the Sky* by Arthur C Clarke. Pages 14-25 were written by Bill Boyle. Pages 90-1 were written by Bill Boyle and Sarah Phillips.

We would like to thank the following for permission to reproduce photographs: Beken of Cowes (UK), pages 17 *above,* 20, 22; British Philatelic Bureau, page 90 (Scottish stamp); J Allan Cash, pages 90, 91; Express Newspapers, pages 15, 17 *below,* 19, 24/25; Rex Features, page 14.

Illustrators, other than those acknowledged with each story, include Peter Foster pp. 24-5; Melissa Webb pp. 66-7; Loui Silvestro pp. 68-71; Bruce Rankin pp. 72-3; Paul Collicutt pp. 90-1.

Contents

The Cellar

Everyone is talking about the cellar, which is what the hole is, an ancient cellar underneath the school, and opened up by the workmen when they started to knock down the Headmaster's old room and the office. It's very old indeed, they say, older than the school itself, probably centuries old, dating back to really ancient buildings that have stood before on that spot, because our school is one of the oldest in the country, and the church we go to was first built by the Saxons in seven hundred and something.

Skeletons, breathes somebody, there are skeletons down there.

"Who says there are?"

"Buggsy's seen them with his own eyes."

"Well, he wouldn't see them with somebody else's, would he?" says Darren, actually drawn out of his reading about space, and taking notice of what's going on here on this planet, for a change.

"Could be Roman skeletons."

"Or Viking. Or skeletons from the cholera epidemic that Sir told us about when nearly half the children in the school died!"

A wail hits the air. "I want to go home, if there's skeletons."

"Don't let me stop you," I say to Heather, as I open the door for her to go. "Yes, the cholera germs do stay with the skeletons and you can catch it easily. And cholera is nearly as bad as rabies. You die in horrible pain."

She is wailing really well as Sir comes in, looking excited.

"Shut up, Heather," he says, and she is so surprised she stops quite still with her mouth wide open.

"Tell us all about it," we say.

"About what?" he grins.

"Skeletons in the cellar."

"What cellar? What skeletons?" But he is still grinning.

"Don't be mean. You know all about it, Sir, because you wrote that book on the history of the school."

"Yes, but I didn't know anything about the cellar then. I didn't know it existed."

"Have you been down there yet, Sir?"

"Yes, I've been down with Mr. Buggit. They're closing it up again quite soon, because they don't think it's safe to leave it open with all the children about."

"Shame. What's it like? Is it haunted?"

"Quiet now. Yes, there are the remains of a few skeletons down there...."

"Oh, oh, oh...."

"Heather, a few old bones won't hurt you...."

Some of the other girls were twitching a bit by now, as well as Heather.

"I knew this school was different," whispers Rosie. "I expect you've been busy in that cellar, Count Dracula."

"How did you guess?" I whisper back.

"Ve 'ave de vays ov finding out," she hisses at me.

"Can you take us down there? Please?"

"I don't want to go. Not with skeletons!"

"Tell us what it's like down there."

"It's older than the school, which is mid-Victorian, and I think it probably dates from late Mediaeval times, like a lot of this city. In one corner there's an interesting arch, which could be even earlier, possibly Norman, and it was in this corner that the workmen discovered the skeletons, three of them actually, buried under a pile of rubble. I am hoping for a few more interesting remains, pots or tools perhaps, we shall have to wait and see. Otherwise, the cellar itself is very dusty and cobwebby, there are some shelves, a few old desks, and an empty cupboard, all Victorian."

"Were you scared when you saw the skeletons?"

"Well, no. I didn't do them any harm and I don't suppose they'll do any to me. You're not scared of the bones your dog chews, are you? Well, I'm not scared of three old skeletons in the school cellar and I hope that you wouldn't be either."

"Who do you think they were?"

"I imagine they were cholera victims, from the epidemic in the eighteen-thirties, probably, when this school, in an earlier building than this, remember, was turned into a hospital, and a great many people died here. Later on the cellar was boarded up for some reason, and then forgotten in time."

"What are they going to do with them?"

"Well, they have to be examined by the official authorities, which always has to happen, no matter how old the bones in question may be. Then they'll probably be buried in peace, the cellar closed up once more, and all trace of today's discovery forgotten."

He sounds as if he is sorry.

"I wish they'd keep it open."

"Yes, it does seem a pity in a way, Gowie, but the

authority have decided that it would be a risk to the
school generally, and we must abide by that."

"Is it haunted, Sir?"

"What, our school? Never."

A low moaning noise is heard from Heather, and this
makes Sir say,

"Come on, back to work," though I bet everybody is
thinking about the skeletons that have been found,

Soon he has us writing about it, trust him, and talking
on tape, giving our ideas on the subject, so that we can
do a school news sheet, asking who we think the
skeletons might have been when they were alive, and
why the cellar was closed like that (that is if you want
to, some kids say it gives them the screaming eebie
jeebies just to think about it at all). But when I take my
story up to Sir, ten pages of it, plus illustrations, ready to
do it up on tape and slides, he says it's the best thing
I've ever done and congratulations.

"It's my sort of subject, that's why," I explain.

"Unfortunately I cannot find skeletons every day in
order to give you inspiration," he grins.

At times, I can see why he's got a giant-sized fan club
in this school. But he's still a teacher and they're berks,
sub-human.

7

At the end of the morning, waiting to be called for dinner, everyone stands jabbering, Rosie and my face forgotten.

"I wonder if it will be in the papers," says Helen Lockey.

"We might be on telly," squeaks Tracy.

"They won't let us near the place," says Simon Singh. "I just been now to take a dekko and they've put a fence around and a notice to say how forbidden it is to enter."

"Oh, they never let us have any fun. I should have liked to explore down there," says JJ.

Coming from the well-known coward, this strikes me as very funny.

"It's easy enough to go down there if you really want to," I say.

"I'd be scared," shivers Heather, looking like a jelly-bellied rhino, "with all the ghosties and bats and spiders and rats down there."

"I don't think any school cellar can be very scary."

"Oh, you're just boasting, Corby," sneers JJ. "You'd be dead scared. Why, when we jumped you, you cried and pretended to be dead..."

"Shut up," snaps Stewpid. "We ain't talking about that."

Rosie, who has been very quiet, listening to all this,

now shows her brace in a toothy grin.

"A whole team on to one person makes anybody play dead. They would be very stupid not to do so."

"You don't know anything about it," JJ snaps. "You've only just come to this school, so you shouldn't go shoving your nose into things you know nothin' about. What I am saying is that Corby is too chicken to go down that cellar, although he says it's easy."

"Pack it in," says Stewpid. "Let's leave it, shall we?"

"You talk a whole load of crap, anyway," I say to JJ. "I don't care whether I go down the cellar or not, it's nothing to me one way or another, all I say is, that if anyone wants to, it's easy."

Mrs. Bond, the dinner lady, starts to line us up.

"However much you boast, I *know* you're chicken," hisses JJ at me.

"Quiet, everybody," cries Mrs. Bond.

"I'll go down there, any time."

"I don't believe you."

"Get knotted, little boy."

"Are you talking to me?" He squares up, fists clenched, and I start to laugh, for he looks very funny.

"Sorry, but you need the rest of the team before you even look like one fighter...."

"Chicken. Chicken." He licks his lips. He's gone barmy.

"Quiet, over there," sings out Mrs. Bond.

"When do I go?"

"Today. Before they close it up."

"O.K."

"You have to bring something out to prove you've been in there, else I shan't believe you."

"Fine. I'll do that small thing."

"You're mad," says Stewpid. "Both of you."

"You're fine, Count Dracula," says Rosie.

"I still say you're chicken," JJ grinds on.

"Look, if I do this, get this idiot off my back for me," I ask Stewpid.

"I'm keeping out of this," says Stewpid. "I've got the team to worry about. The doctor says I can play again next week."

Dinner is meatballs and rice, followed by ginger pud. I sit by Rosie, and instead of giving Heather a bit of fun which is what I usually do at dinner-time, Rosie and I plan strategy. I have to keep out of sight of Buggsy and the workmen. And see that JJ doesn't tell tales to somebody, so Rosie says she'll stick to him like glue. Dinner over, I wander round to the forbidden area, and sure enough it's knocking off time, half of the workmen aren't there, and the rest are drinking their tea in the tin hut.

I run to the playground tree, and flatten myself against it, then run from there to the hole, like Starsky and Hutch. The blank gaping hole welcomes me. The fence is nothing, it wouldn't stop a flea, let alone me.

It's dark inside, just as I thought it would be. First I jump down the stairs that have been boarded up for years, run swiftly down and turn out of sight from the world above. Here it's plenty dark, with no movement or sound at all, the only light a sliver from that opened up bit where I came in. The air smells stuffy and thick as I move forward slowly, hands out in front, ready to encounter trouble, ready to protect myself from anything at all that may be lurking, anything that may have stayed down there from when it had all been first locked up, all those years ago. And for the first time I really do wonder why it was locked up, what for? And I shiver a bit, but

not much, for the dark's my friend, and has been for a
long time now. Only, I wish Boris was with me. Boris is
usually with me when I go exploring in the dark. His
whiskers twitch beside me. But here I am alone. And I
can't help wondering, as I move slowly forward, if the
cellar was boarded up because it wasn't safe, or because
something had to be boarded up down here because it
was ... dangerous ... and those thoughts are dangerous
so I push them away and watch carefully what I am
doing.

I'm getting used to the dark now, and can see much
better. The room is large, with a low ceiling above, and a
grating at the far end, so bunged up with dirt and
cobwebs that only a pale ray of light straggles through.
The floor is stone, uneven and dirty. In the corner are a
couple of old desks with iron feet and lift-up lids and
seats, like the ones they had in schools long ago, with a
pile of clothes on the floor beside them. I stir the clothes
with my feet as there might just be a ratty friend there, a
cousin of Boris. But nothing is in the clothes nor in the
desks when I peep inside, only an old smell that seems as
if it gathers up and moves away, and a fat spider
scuttling into the distance. "I shan't hurt you," I tell it.

I turn to the corner with the arch Sir spoke of. There
it is in the gloom, rounded above the rubble, but there
are no white bones, no skeletons. They've gone. Pity. I
should've liked to see those. It is all quiet and sad,
somehow. I look around for something to take back,
there's an empty inkwell in the desk — they must have
had fun throwing ink at each other in the old days — I
take one, and there's a scrubbing brush with half its
bristles missing, a broken globe, and an old clock with
Roman numerals, stopped at twelve o'clock. Midday?
Midnight? I stop and listen as something stirs on the
edge of my hearing and is gone again. I'd better get a
move on. The tea break will be over soon, and I must get
out of here. As I turn to go a small cupboard catches my
eye. I open the door. It is empty, except ... except for a
key, old, ordinary. I pick it up and push it into my pocket
and close the door. Then I turn to leave.

11

And for a minute I do not know where to get out of
the cellar.

And I am afraid, terrified, I have the feeling that the
cellar does not want me to go, it wants to keep me for
company in its age-long loneliness, and I am so scared I
break out in a sweat, despite the fact that it is autumn
and cold underground, and my heart is pounding so loud
that I can't think, think, think, go on, think, you know the
way out of here, it's quite light really, then where has the
entrance gone?

And it's there, just where it was all the time, and I don't know why I was afraid, after all, I like the dark and I like cellars, I'm used to them, let's get out of here, fast, Gowie, you've done what you said you'd do and you've got something to prove it, let's go, go....

I head for the great outside, and straight into Buggsy, who just by chance is waiting by the tree....

"Funny it should be you," he says. "Come on, let's go and visit the Headmaster."

He stands me in front of a large notice saying, ALL CHILDREN MUST STAY AWAY FROM THIS AREA. IT IS DANGEROUS.

"Pity you never learned to read," he says.

I have to write out two hundred words beginning with B, and their meanings. I know quite a lot of rude words beginning with B, but I'm not allowed to use *them*. Rosie slips in to help me with a few. She is bothered because JJ managed to get away from her trailing him, when he went to the bogs. She thinks he came out the other side and then told Buggsy I was in the cellar.

I'm not bothered. At the end of the afternoon, nearly everyone from all the fourth year comes to look at the key and the inkwell, and I give a talk, describing the cellar and How I Felt in There. JJ walks away looking green and stupid, as the crowd gathers round.

Only at the end do I see Sir detach himself from a corner and walk away, as well. He's carrying the cassette recorder.

"Makes a good tape," he grins. "Thanks, Corby."

Written by Gene Kemp
Illustrated by Sara Woodward

Woman of the Sea
Clare Francis

Clare Francis was born in Surbiton, Surrey in 1946. Her favourite time of year as a youngster was the summer, which was spent by her family on the Isle of Wight. It was there that she learned to sail. She began crewing for her father in his dinghy at the age of seven. "At nine, I started crewing the local champion and from then I spent every summer in boats."

At the age of thirteen, Clare was sent to the Royal Ballet School. Her time there taught her perseverance which was so necessary later in her life.

Throughout her teenage years, Clare continued to spend all her spare time in boats. By this time, she had her own small, wooden dinghy, which helped to increase her experience of sailing.

When she left London University, Clare worked for a few
years in marketing. Then, at the age of twenty-six, decided
to travel. She begged and borrowed enough money to buy a
32-foot cruiser called *Gulliver G*.

With some friends, Clare planned a world cruise in the
boat, working on the way, but gradually all the friends
dropped out. "Very well, I said, I'll go on my own. So I went
on my own, from England to Newport, Rhode Island, in the
summer of 1973."

After returning to England, Clare took part in the 1974
two-handed Round Britain Race. With Eve Bonham as her
partner, they were the first ever all-woman crew to enter
the race. The pair were delighted when they finished third
out of the sixty-five boats which had started the race.

In 1975, Clare entered the Azores and Back Singlehanded Race in a 38-foot sloop, *Robertson's Golly*. The boat was sponsored by Robertson's jam and marmalade firm, one of Clare's earlier employers. Clare's boat came tenth out of a total of fifty.

With these experiences of ocean racing behind her, Clare Francis decided to enter the most difficult singlehanded race of all, the Transatlantic Singlehanded Race. This race is held every four years and Clare decided to enter the 1976 event. She was the first British woman to take part in this most dangerous of races.

Clare again decided to use *Robertson's Golly* as her craft, and the 38-foot sloop was proudly loaned to her by Joan and Ron Green, its owners. At 5 foot 2 inches tall, and weighing only seven and a half stone, Clare was by far the smallest competitor in the race. In fact, she is the smallest person ever to have sailed the Atlantic alone, and she did it in one of the world's toughest races.

When the Transatlantic Race began on 5th June, 1976, Clare Francis had 2,800 miles of sea in front of her. The journey from Plymouth to Newport, Rhode Island is one of the most dangerous that the singlehanded sailor can attempt. Among the problems that are likely to be met are icebergs, fog, gales and storms. It is also vital to be watchful for shipping in this busy area of the North Atlantic.

Besides trying to keep her boat on course in the rough weather, Clare was also kept busy doing other things during the race. She was filming the drama of her own race for the BBC, and had to manage camera and sound equipment singlehanded. When the documentary was shown in October 1976 it showed clearly the problems that Clare had encountered on her dangerous voyage.

Clare was also kept busy sending radio reports of her race to a daily newspaper and writing notes about her adventure. These notes later became her first book, *Come Hell or High Water*.

Like the other competitors in the race, Clare survived some terrible Atlantic weather. This included two weeks in a 'blanket' of fog, two violent storms, and the shock of waking up one morning to find that the boat had just sailed between two massive icebergs while she slept. If the boat had hit them, it would have sunk immediately.

One hundred and twenty-five boats left Plymouth, but only seventy-eight finished the trip. In the dreadful weather, forty boats had to retire from the race, five competitors were rescued from their sinking boats and two experienced sailors were drowned.

Having the skill and good fortune to survive the storms, Clare was the first woman to reach the finishing line in the race. Not only that, but she beat the previous women's record by more than three days. She was also the first British competitor, male or female, to finish in a conventional, single-hulled yacht.

The 1976 Transatlantic Race saw the worst weather in the history of the event. That year the race had the largest number of boats starting that it had ever had, but over a third of them failed to finish the course. Conditions were so dangerous that two of the competitors lost their lives.

"When you lose a friend, all those marvellous parties at the other end don't feel right."

The race did have its tragedy, and Clare was very upset by the death of her friend, Mike McMullen, lost with his boat *Three Cheers*.

In August 1977, Clare Francis became the first woman skipper of a boat in the Round the World Race. With her husband, the yachtsman Jacques Redon among the crew, she entered in the sixty-five-foot *ADC Accutrac*.

The *ADC Accutrac* had twenty-seven sails — all of which needed repairing during the race. The interior of the boat was divided into three main cabins and a saloon. However, with twelve people on board, it was very crowded and only nine could sleep at any one time.

The race for the Whitbread Trophy consisted of a 27,000 mile journey round the world, sailing from west to east, via the three Capes. Only boats which were between forty-five and eighty feet in length were allowed to enter. The *ADC Accutrac* had fourteen rivals to beat in the 1977 race.

The race started on Saturday 27th August which was a grey, gloomy day. *ADC Accutrac* left Portsmouth harbour with hundreds of spectator boats cheering the crews on their way. The first leg of 5,800 miles was the shortest stage of the race. On the very first day several sails were torn in high winds, and the following day the radio aerial broke away from the top of the mast: not the best of beginnings. Averaging about 158 miles a day, *Accutrac* arrived in Cape Town on 9th October, in ninth position in the race.

After two weeks of repair work on the boat, *Accutrac* left Cape Town on 25th October. This second leg of 7,400 miles took five weeks and one day, through strong winds and thick fog. Wearily, Clare and her crew arrived in Auckland on 29th November, now in seventh place. They spent Christmas in New Zealand, before restarting on Boxing Day.

The 7,400 mile leg from Auckland to Rio was probably the most dangerous stage of the race. The threat of icebergs made everyone doubly watchful, and the wild seas and enormous waves shook those who were sleeping out of their bunks. Rounding Cape Horn, they were met by Force 12 winds, blowing at 70 knots. Everybody on board was seasick, feeling miserable and having to work strapped in harness, for fear of being washed overboard. *Accutrac* finally, gratefully, arrived in Rio on 31st January, having battled into fifth place in the race.

Clare and her crew left Rio on 22nd February 1978 with 5,500 miles in front of them for Portsmouth and home. The equator was crossed again, and one of the many memorable sights was that of shoals of flying fish alongside the boat. *Accutrac* beat *Flyer*, the winner of the Trophy, on this final leg, and reached Portsmouth on 28th March. At the end of the 27,000 mile race, Clare Francis had led her crew round the world to finish in fifth place in the most difficult sailing event possible.

Despite the discomfort of the cramped boat, Clare was determined not to waste the seven months that the journey took. She recorded a film for the BBC during the race, sent reports back for radio broadcast in Britain, wrote articles for a Sunday newspaper and made the notes for her book about the race, *Come Wind or Weather*.

After the Whitbread race, Clare Francis spent the next three years lecturing, writing and working on the BBC series, *The Commanding Sea*. The series showed the enormous size, fearful power and mysterious depths of the sea, and man's struggle to conquer it. Clare made six very different voyages of discovery to provide material for her book and the six films that made up *The Commanding Sea*. Subjects included the ancient trade routes, the original sea explorers, life in the deep sea and naval power through the ages.

For one of her journeys on film, Clare joined the crew on the replica of the *Golden Hind*. The original ship, captained by Sir Francis Drake, was the second ship to sail round the world. This replica had been built in 1973 to circumnavigate the globe in celebration of the four hundredth anniversary of Drake's voyage. Clare, and camera crew, joined the ship for part of the journey through the South China Sea to Singapore.

The last of Clare's filmed voyages was made in the *Alvin*, and took her 6,000 feet — over a mile — below the sea's surface. The *Alvin* is a submarine, or more correctly, a submersible. In appearance the *Alvin* looks more like an insect than a boat, with its short body, a tail which supports a large propeller, antennae and sensors, and its two clawlike arms which can pick objects off the seabed. Clare's dive in *Alvin* was made off Nassau, in the Bahamas.

"Sailing was lovely while it lasted. But when you go to the limits of yourself, look fear full in the face and see the possibility of dying, you've gone over the edge of experience and don't want to do it again." Clare Francis. The death of Clare's friend, Mike McMullen in the 1976 Transatlantic race, left a deep scar, and was one of the main reasons why Clare decided to retire from racing.

Inspired by some of the stories that she had discovered while doing research for *The Commanding Sea*, Clare thought of writing a novel. Two years of further research and writing followed which resulted, in 1983, in the publication of *Night Sky*. This proved to be an international bestseller, being published and praised in twenty-two countries and in thirteen languages.

In October 1985, Clare followed up her first novel by publishing *Red Crystal*, a political thriller, full of suspense and action.

Her years of racing and sea exploration behind her, Clare Francis is now settled in her new career as a writer of adventure novels. Of her sailing days she remembers, "some unforgettable experiences, but also boredom, discomfort and longing for home."

QUAKA RAJA

There was once a poor widow who lived in a hut at the edge of the forest with her four children.

She favoured her three daughters — Minnie Minnie, Minnie Bitana, and Philambo — but she did not care a wit for her son, Quaka Raja. Yet Quaka Raja was obedient and worked hard in the vegetable garden in front of the hut while his three sisters quarelled and fought among themselves all day. They made fun of Quaka because he was kind to the birds and animals of the forest, and always saved some of his food for them.

Every Friday the widow set out for the village market where she sold the vegetables and fruit from her garden. Everyone flocked to buy her dasheen, yams, sweet potatoes, mangoes, sapodillas, peas and beans, and soon her basket was empty. With the money she received she bought food to take home and filled her basket with all manner of goodies. There was Arape, a cornmeal pancake with spicy meat filling, molasses balls, sugar cakes, black pudding, and many other things besides.

When she returned to the little hut she stood outside and sang:

"Minnie Minnie, come here,
Minnie Bitana, come here,
Philambo, come here,
Leave Quaka Raja one dey."

As soon as the three daughters heard the song they ran to unlock the door, pushing Quaka Raja aside as the mother did not want him. Then the food was shared. But Quaka Raja's portion was always the least of all.

27

Now in the forest lived a man called Zobolak who was feared by all the villagers. He was a hideous-looking creature, with a deeply scarred face, fiery red eyes, and arms and legs that were huge and round, with clawlike hands and feet. Mothers warned their children to keep away from the forest, for whenever a child disappeared it was whispered that Zobolak had stolen it, though no one could prove this was true.

One Friday, when the widow returned from market, Zobolak, who had been hunting agouti, happened to be nearby. Peeping through the bushes he heard the widow's song and saw the three daughters run out to greet their mother. Zobolak could hardly restrain himself from rushing forward and seizing the three girls then and there, but he was as cunning as the wild animals which he hunted in the forest. He settled down to wait.

The next Friday the widow again set out for market. After some time had passed, Zobolak crept up to the hut and sang in a high voice:

"Minnie Minnie, come here,
Minnie Minnie, come here,
Minnie Minnie, come here,
Leave Quaka Raja one dey."

The three daughters ran to open the door, but Quaka Raja said, "Sisters, sisters, do not go out. That is not Mamma's song." And he stood in front of the door and would not let them out even though they tugged and pulled until they were exhausted.

When the children did not open the door, Zobolak hid in the forest until the mother returned. But he stayed close by to listen carefully to the song.

The following Friday the mother set off once more for the village, and after a little while Zobolak crept up to the hut and sang in a high voice:

"Minnie Minnie, come here,
Minnie Minnie, come here,
Philambo, come here,
Leave Quaka Raja one dey."

The three daughters ran to unlock the door, but Quaka Raja said, "Sisters, sisters, do not go out. That is not Mamma's song."

They tugged and pulled and scratched him but he stood fast in front of the door, and at last they fell down exhausted.

Once more Zobolak crept away into the forest when they did not open the door, but he waited close by until the mother returned.

At last Friday came. Zobolak's eyes gleamed with excitement as he waited. No sooner had the widow left than he crept up to the hut and sang in a high voice:

"Minnie, Minnie, come here,
Minnie Bitana, come here,
Philambo, come here,
Leave Quaka Raja one dey."

Quaka Raja stood in front of the door and begged his sisters not to go out. Their mother had just left. How could she be back so soon? But they tugged and pulled and scratched and kicked him so hard that he fell to the ground, senseless.

They ran out to greet their mother, but — "Ayayayayay!" — there was Zobolak waiting for them. He threw them into his sack, slung it over his shoulder and off he went into the forest where he lived.

By the time Quaka Raja came to his senses Zobolak was far, far away. Quaka Raja ran hither and yon calling his sisters, but only the birds cheeped back at him. When his mother returned from the village and he told her what had happened, she was wild with grief. But Quaka Raja said, "Do not cry, Mamma, I will go and look for my sisters and bring them back to you."

At first his mother begged him not to go. "Son, you are all that I have now," she said; "I cannot lose you too." 31

But Quaka Raja pleaded with her until she agreed.
So she packed him some of the food she had brought
back and sent him off with tears in her eyes.

Quaka walked long and he walked far. He walked
all day, and as night fell he saw a light in the distance.
As he approached it he came to a hut half hidden by
trees and creepers. Inside he could hear his sisters
crying.

What to do? He could not rescue them without help.
As he stood under a tree thinking, an owl overhead
hooted and nearly frightened him out of his wits. At
that moment he thought of a plan. He could ask his
friends, the birds and animals of the forest, to help him.

Much later that night, as the moon climbed down behind the mountain, the stillness of the forest was shattered by a horrible noise. Zobolak was startled out of his sleep as the sound grew louder and louder and came nearer and nearer, like the shrieks of a hundred demons coming after him. He rushed out of his hut like a hunted animal and ran deep into the forest, over the mountains, anywhere away from that terrible noise.

What was that noise? It was the sound of owls hooting, frogs croaking, wild cats yowling, wild pigs snorting and grunting, parrots screaming and birds chirping and whistling. They had all come to help Quaka Raja.

So Quaka Raja returned home with his sisters and his mother was so proud of him that if he weren't such a sensible child he would have been thoroughly spoiled.

And for all we know Zobolak is still running!

Written by Grace Hallworth
Illustrated by Nicola Heindl

Who was Achilles?

Mighty war hero that's who and main character in the story of the Trojan war. This adventure known as the *Iliad* was written by the Greek poet Homer around 700 B.C. and it leaves today's soap operas for dead, especially the part about Achilles.

Achilles was born to Peleus and a water goddess named Thetis. Like any likely lad, he becomes the apple of his mum's eye. So, when Thetis hears that her lusty son could be made invulnerable by dipping him in the river Styx she takes the bawling infant by his heel and plunges him into the water. Too bad for Achilles that it didn't occur to his mum that she really should have submerged ALL of her child.

Time goes by and Achilles, like all proper heroes, grows up handsome and brave. He becomes a mighty hunter who can also play a musical instrument, sing and dance. In other words, he fast becomes the most eligible young man in Greece — but he can't cut loose from mum's apron strings.

Meanwhile, the Trojan War is about to begin. The King of Troy's son, Paris, has been stupid enough to run off with Helen, wife of Menelaus, King of Sparta. (I told you it was like a soap opera!)

your heel, Achilles?

Thetis, being a goddess, knows that Achilles will die if he fights in this war, so she packs the young adolescent off to the court of yet another king, disguised as a girl! (You can see how much he was under his mother's thumb!)

The plot thickens. It's time to meet Odysseus . He's another king and a big man in Greece. Against his better judgement he's been drawn into fighting on Menelaus's side and he's decided he'll have a better chance of surviving if he has Achilles as his right hand man. Gossip being what it is, he hears rumours about the boy's whereabouts, so he disguises himself as a door-to-door salesman and pops into the court where Achilles (still disguised as a girl) is languishing amongst the maidens. Odysseus hands out jewels and scarves to the maidens and he watches to see who shows least interest in them. Odysseus then offers some daggers and swords, and Achilles betrays himself by handling them like a man. Odysseus puts the hard word on him to join the army. Achilles, who has been told that his fate is either to win glory and die young, or to have a long dull existence, decides to opt for a short life and a merry one, and off they go together to test his courage on the battlefield.

The story gets pretty complicated after that, but in the end after ten long years of siege and fighting, when most of the main characters are polished off, Paris (who should have been ashamed of himself for starting all the fuss) wounds Achilles in (you've guessed it) — his heel, the only part of him that's not sword or dagger proof. The arrow is poisoned, so that's it! Ring down the curtain on Achilles!

Why should we remember him?

To start with, part of you is named after him. The tendon that connects the muscles of your calf to your heelbone is called your Achilles tendon. (It's the one most often strained or hurt in athletes.) Also, you're sure to strike reference to a person's "Achilles heel" at some stage. It's used when the speaker is describing someone's weak spot, the thing that makes her or him vulnerable. A "small, but fatal weakness" is the dictionary definition.

LOOK BEFORE YOU LEAP!

Retold from Aesop's fable, "The Fox and the Goat"
by **PAT EDWARDS**. Illustrated by **PETER FOSTER**.

One day, a fox, who'd stopped for a quick drink from a well, slipped off the edge and fell in...

The fox tried to climb up the walls but they were too slippery.

Perhaps an Olympic-style jump might do it!

She tried jumping but the walls were just too high.

The fox rested, trying to think of another plan.

Cut steps into the wall? No knife! Float up holding a balloon? No balloon! Stand on a box? No box!

37

Just then a goat came by.

Boy! Am I ever thirsty! Thank goodness I found a well!

The wily fox decided not to let on that she was in trouble.

Hello there! How's the water?

It's so good, I hopped right in so I could really wallow!

It's much easier to drink my fill down here.

SLURP!

Come on in. The water's fine!

Without stopping to think, the goat leapt into the well.

Just what I needed!

Certainly it's nice and cool!

There goes the neighbourhood!

Quick as a flash the fox jumped up on the goat's horns.

Hey! What's happening?

There goes the fox!

If you had as much brain as you have beard, you wouldn't have jumped in!

Next time, look before you leap!

Maa-aa-aa-Help!

It's no test of courage to rush into things before thinking of the consequences. ALWAYS LOOK BEFORE YOU LEAP!

39

UNDYARNING
Daughter of
The Great Water

When Edward Curr was twenty-one, his father gave him the task of establishing sheep runs in the new colony of Port Phillip. The year was 1841 and the young man was excited by the chance to explore the Murray River. Edward meets up with a small group of Aborigines from the Towroonban tribe. When he discovers one who has already adopted a European name, he decides to hire Tommy and his canoe.

Tommy proves an able guide. Edward learns that the Aborigines of the area call the river "Tongala, the Great Water" and that his part of it is home to the Yota Yota, one of the groups that make up the Bangerang tribe which numbers more than a thousand people. He also hears of Pekka the Bunyip who delights in eating small children.

The canoe was a big one, of family size, six metres long, made from a single sheet of thick redgum bark. Across the bow was a clay hearth where Tommy could grill a fish or a duck. In front of the hearth Tommy had placed an armful of couch grass for the white man to sit on. He made no comment when his passenger kept his firestick in his hand, holding it across his knees.

The redgums overhung the stream, many of them showing the oval scars where canoes had been peeled off. Some of these gnarled trees with great swellings of knots like huge warts on the trunks could have been a thousand years old. From their high branches, the white crane, the blue crane, and the nankeen bird stared down inquisitively. *Wigilopka* — the laughing jackass — cackled over their heads. It was the time of the low river and the shallows were clear. Once the white man saw a codfish peep out from his home in a sunken log.

"Grow big like wallaby," Tommy said proudly. Proud because everything in the river belonged to the black people, and there was no better fish. "Fat good."

40

With a wave of his hand he demonstrated how the oil from the fish was good to rub on bodies and heads.

They passed a bough fish-trap standing half out of the water. Tommy said the Yota Yota built the trap in the dry months. In winter, when the river was high, shoals of fish were spotted from their canoes and driven into the trap where they were easily taken. The Bangerang people were all fine swimmers and in summer it was enjoyable to enter the water with their barbed spears and pursue their next meal. In winter when the water was cold and discoloured by flood, the fish were difficult to spear and then the traps helped greatly.

This well-fed Towroonban was tall, straight and broad. His long rowing-pole was strong against the current, the muscles in his arms and legs and back working in shining black unison.

As they rounded one of the many bends, they surprised the fishing-party. Instantly the tossed laughter and chatter ceased. Silence.

Tommy said, "Not pleased. Not know you come."

Edward grinned to himself. He should have sent his message stick.

Now the cry of fear and warning rose high to the overhanging trees.

"*Yuk-ki! Yuk-ki!*"

Children stopped spearing frogs. Tadpoles escaped into the current. Adults went rigid. But only for a moment. Swift as a shower of spears the canoes thrust into shore, and the swimmers thrashed out for the bank. Old men shouted orders, women screamed to their children.

"*Yuk-ki*. Ooo-oh! Hurry! Ooo-oh . . . hurry!"

Never before had this group seen a white man. But they recognised both the white face and the weapon they had been told about. They knew the firestick made a great bang and then killed a black fellow from a far greater distance than any spear could be thrown.

Safety lay in the bush beyond the camp. They poled and swam and climbed and ran to this safety.

Under the trees small fires were smouldering. Woven baskets and fishing-nets hung from the branches. This was an important camp site. With a plentiful supply of food always in the river or on its banks, the tribes gathered here for feasting, exchange of goods, corroboree and ritual. Many generations had raised the cooking ovens to big calcined mounds on the river bank.

The women grabbed up their babies, and the old men snatched spears or possum-skin cloaks as they fled. All made directly for trees and scrub.

Undyarning swung a two-year-old boy on to her back. She ran with him up the slightly sloping bank, passing the evenly spaced, semi-circular mia-mias of leaf and stick, all facing the same way with backs to the wind, each the shelter of one family. She skirted the wafting blue smoke of the cooking fires, helter-skelter, bare feet firm on the rough ground.

Tommy laughed at the scamper of his kinsmen. He shouted to reassure them. Told them that the white man was friendly, that he would not harm them and to sit down. He gave them time to listen by slackening the speed of his craft.

But no one sat down. Soon nothing moved on the bank but the blue spirals of smoke, and the turn of a leaf in air disturbed by the rush of the escapees. Once behind the leaves the noise stilled. Even the wails of the small boy that Undyarning had whisked away from the white man were stilled to the quiet of the morning haze.

Nothing moved, except one very old man. He remained on the bank, at the water's edge, straight as old bones would straighten, watching the white man come.

The canoe moved slowly but delicately on the water. Skimming as lightly as a leaf across the ripples of the current.

Tommy lifted his pole to point at the old fellow. "Him — father-belong-Warri."

"An ancient," said Edward.

"Him bin best hunter. Best spear fisherman. Best Law man. That fella — very old."

Tommy didn't dare name the old one, except as "father-belong-Warri". Names were sacred, with many taboos regarding their use or non-use. To call a man by his name might mean his return to haunt you at death. And the Bangerang, and the Towroonban, and the Wongatpan, were nervous always of Pekka — ghosts.

The young white sheep-man knew of Warri, the Bangerang black who was, himself, a grandfather. Edward estimated that this old fellow, Warri's father, must be near ninety. It said much for the food productiveness of the area, that these *Moira* blacks could have so many children, and so many elderly members of the tribe. Where a tribe had to move constantly in search of food, there were always fewer children, and people seldom lived to be truly old. The *Moira* was good country.

The black man stood naked. His possum-skin cloak lay with his other spears and woven bags farther up the bank. It had a design of the emu chase in red ochre on the skin side.

His black head was shiny bald but he had a long white beard. The white hair, like fluffs of wild cotton, hid the scars of manhood raised on his chest so long ago. Clenched in his fist was his barbed fishing spear.

The old fellow did not turn and run with the women. He confronted the canoe, as though he were the whole tribe — defied the white man, even when the white man stood up in the boat, gun in hand.

Tommy the pole-man slowed the speed of his craft further, allowing it to drift broadside-on towards the bank. And for him too, now, there was uncertainty and fear. What had he brought to his people?

The women broke silence then. "Ooo-oh — come, old one! Hurry! Hurry!"

They entreated him, wailed to him, but he stood there. He shook his spear at the white man. He screeched to him to leave the river and the fish and the turtle and the possum to the black man, to whom they belonged. "I hate you, white man! I spit on you! I spear you!"

He leapt up and down in warlike capers, feet thumping the earth, spear cleaving the air. His abuse screamed across the water.

The women and the other old men feared for his life. The white man's firestick would surely bang now. They pleaded with father-belong-Warri to come away before it was too late.

"Ooo-oh — come, old one! Come! You old fellow — you die!"

Then as the boat neared the bank they pushed a young girl — Undyarning — out from the safety of the trees.

"Go!" they commanded her. "Bring the old one to safety!"

She was no more than ten. Her slightly wavy hair was matted around her head and she was wearing now a possum-skin cloak fastened about her shoulders with a pin of sharpened bone. She held back. She tried to resist the hands pushing her from the safety of the trees. Many hands there were to urge her forward.

"That one — Undyarning," Tommy informed the squatter. He could say her name because she was young and a girl. And he was glad to speak and take the attention of the white man.

"Girl," Tommy said again.

Perhaps the tribe had heard that the white man did not make war on children, even though they killed the black man with no more thought than they rid themselves of the pestilent kangaroo. Perhaps they reasoned that, if they were to lose anyone in this rescue attempt, it had better be a girl who was not as important or valuable as a boy.

Undyarning hung back and resisted until pushed right out into the open. Then she stood still for a moment, slender as any of the reeds of the river bank and as straight, as though taking stock of the task she had been given, stock of the white man in the canoe and the black man at the water's edge, and of herself, a black girl, sent to thwart the intent of both. Then she started forward, past the mia-mias and the cooking fires, taking a direct line for the old hunter.

Because Edward was young, with a still-thin beard, he saw how he could impress these people with the power of the weapon in his hand. Some of them — not this tribe perhaps — had already proved a nuisance around the station, stealing sheep when they fancied mutton. If he was going to obtain a squatting licence on this bit of country, it was as well to establish authority now. He raised his gun. In the next few minutes they would live in agony for the fate of the grandfather, and for Undyarning.

Edward sighted the gun at the girl. His finger reached for the trigger. Even these unsophisticated people must know that, if he fired at such close range, he must kill.

Tommy clutched his pole. He wanted to push off yet he, too, feared the firestick.

The child, not many metres distant, saw the white man's sighting of his gun. There was a brief hesitation, a momentary break in the rhythm of her movement, but she didn't alter course. She came forward steadily, walking, not running, her eyes looking straight into the white man's face, and at the gun. She pulled her possum skin tight as she neared him.

She had to pass close in front of the gun to reach the old man. Her eyes revealed her uncertainty. Would it bang — would blue smoke leap — would she die?

Large dark eyes — frightened, yet she came on. She knew what she had to do. The grandfather had to be taken by the hand. No matter if she died, she had to try. There was no retreat to the safety of the trees. The tribe had pushed her out to do this. No matter if she died, she would try to take father-belong-Warri by the hand.

She passed directly in front of the white man and his weapon. If she quivered as she passed, the possum-skin did not quiver. She reached the old one who was still thumping bony feet and cursing in his Yota Yota tongue.

She spoke to him in a soft voice and stretched up high to pull his hand down to hers. She had to catch hold of it as it lowered in one of its wild declamatory sweeps. She clasped the pink palm, gripped it tight. She pressed it into her side, holding it close to her. Her voice and touch seemed at once to quieten the old fellow. He stopped thumping his bony feet and the Yota Yota curse died in his throat.

For a moment they were both still, the girl and the grandfather. Gently then she turned him away from the river and the gun — turned, so that both their backs were to the white man. She continued to speak to the grandfather soft words of their tribe, but she didn't urge him to run.

Undyarning walked father-belong-Warri away as steadily as she had walked towards him. The old man followed her lead without question, becoming again the frail, dependent old man that he was and together they walked quietly to the shelter of the trees, never looking back.

The young man with the gun at his shoulder watched them go until, once again, nothing moved on the river bank.

He was impressed. He was ashamed. "Come," he said to Tommy. "I've frightened them enough."

Tommy was relieved to pole his shallow craft, which floated like a huge gumleaf with puckered-up edges, out into the middle of the stream. The Great Water carried the canoe. Piled against the curve ahead was the debris of a thousand floods. Fallen redgums, whose wood was nearly as hard as iron and rotted so slowly, snagged the river into ripples. But the fretwork roots of the living trees were an exposed clamp on the steep banks. Their trunks were painted in grand whorls of grey and yellow like the streaks of corroboree; their shaggy black butts were giant bellies; their lifting branches were muscled arms.

As the canoe slid away around the bend, gliding quickly past the waterhole where Bekka lived, the young squatter sat again on his cushion of couch grass and held his gun across his knees.

"That girl — she took the old man, and they walked away . . ." he marvelled softly. "She didn't know whether I would shoot or not."

The Towroonban was able to smile again.

"Undyarning — what control she showed, what courage . . ."

Tommy was pleased indeed that Undyarning had so impressed the white man. And he sent his craft forward through that debris of centuries with the great skill and surety learned by his tribe through those centuries.

Yes, Undyarning had courage. Edward Micklethwaite Curr always retained respect and sympathy for the Aboriginal people. But it was not so with many of the settlers who quickly followed him to those rich pastures. Most of them were interested only in getting a grip on the land, especially the river banks. The Aborigines who had fished, swum, and lived on the river they had called Tongala — the Great Water — for 30 000 years, were hunted and harassed out of their way. Many of the black people died.

But from the remnants of the Yota Yota tribe was to come a very famous Aboriginal son, Sir Douglas Ralph Nicholls. He was born and grew up on the banks of the Murray River and became a great footballer, boxer and runner, a pastor of the Church of Christ and, lastly, Governor of South Australia. And — who knows? — it is not impossible for Undyarning to have been his great-grandmother.

Written by Mavis Thorpe Clarke
Illustrated by John Fairbridge

SPACE PIRATES

Hi! My name is Ron. Karl, Tim and myself, all work Station in space. It's a busy come and go, on visits to and from Earth and the surrounding planets.

My friends Peter and as apprentices on Earth's Inner station where all kinds of spacecraft

This story began when Peter, who is always reading stories about space pirates or watching T V programmes about them, became convinced that the spacecraft Cygnus was acting suspiciously. He persuaded Karl to take one of the shuttles out to investigate Cygnus. Tim and myself remained on the Station, in radio contact, listening to Peter and Karl on a loudspeaker in our workshop.

Although they could find nothing suspicious as they manoeuvred their shuttle around the exterior of Cygnus, Tim was determined to open the cargo hatch. Next we heard a muffled "clank", then a shriek . . . ! We didn't help matters by shouting our own queries, and it was some time before Tim restored order.

"Stop yelling, everybody! Now, Peter, tell us exactly what you've found."

I could hear Peter give a sort of gulp as he collected his breath.

"This ship is full of *guns*!" he gasped. "Honest — I'm, not fooling! I can see about twenty of them, clipped to the walls. And they're not like any guns I've ever seen before. They've got funny nozzles and there are red and green cylinders fixed beneath them. I can't imagine what they're supposed — "

"Karl!" Tim ordered. "Is Peter pulling our legs?"

"No," came the reply. "It's perfectly true. I don't like to say this, but if there *are* such things as ray-guns, we're looking at them now."

"What shall we do?" wailed Peter. He didn't seem at all happy at finding this support for his theories.

"Don't touch anything!" ordered Tim. "Give us a detailed description of everything you can see, and then come straight back."

But before Peter could obey, we all had a second and much worse shock. For suddenly we heard Karl gasp: "What's that?" There was silence for a moment: then a voice I could hardly recognize as Peter's whispered: "There's a ship outside. It's connecting up. What shall we do?"

"Make a run for it," whispered Tim urgently — as if whispering made any difference. "Shoot out of the lock as quickly as you can and come back to the Station by different routes. It's dark for another ten minutes — they probably won't see you."

"Too late," said Karl, still hanging on to the last shreds of his composure. "They're already coming aboard. There goes the outer door now."

For a moment no one could think of anything to say. Then Tim, still whispering, breathed into the microphone: "Keep calm! If you tell them that you're in radio contact with us, they won't dare touch you."

This, I couldn't help thinking, was being rather optimistic. Still, it might be good for our companions' morale, which was probably at a pretty low ebb.

"I'm going to grab one of those guns," Peter called. "I don't know how they work, but it may scare them. Karl, you take one as well."

"For heaven's sake be careful!" warned Tim, now looking very worried. He turned to me.

"Ron, call the Commander and tell him what's happening — quickly! And get a telescope on the *Cygnus* to see what ship's over there."

We should have thought of this before, of course, but it had been forgotten in the general excitement.

"They're in the control room now," reported Peter, "I can see them. They're not wearing space-suits, and they aren't carrying guns. That gives us quite an advantage."

I suspected that Peter was beginning to feel a little happier, wondering if he might yet be a hero.

"I'm going out to meet them," he announced suddenly. "It's better than waiting in here, where they're bound to find us. Come on, Karl."

We waited breathlessly. I don't know what we expected — anything, I imagine, from a salvo of shots to the hissing or crackling of whatever mysterious weapons our friends were carrying. The one thing we didn't anticipate was what actually happened.

We heard Peter say (and I give him full credit for sounding quite calm): "What are you doing here, and who are you?"

There was silence for what seemed an age. I could picture the scene as clearly as if I'd been present — Peter and Karl standing at bay behind their weapons, the men they had challenged wondering whether to surrender or to make a fight for it.

Then, unbelievably, someone laughed. There were a few words we couldn't catch, in what seemed to be English, but they were swept away by a roar of merriment. It sounded as if three or four people were all laughing simultaneously, at the tops of their voices.

We could do nothing but wait and wonder until the tumult had finished. Then a new voice, sounding amused and quite friendly, came from the speaker.

"O.K., boys — you might as well put those gadgets down. You couldn't kill a mouse with them unless you swatted it over the head. I guess you're from the Station. If you want to know who we are, this is Twenty-First Century Films, at your service. I'm Lee Thomson, assistant producer. And those ferocious weapons you've got are the ones that Props made for our new interstellar epic. I'm glad to know they've convinced *somebody* — they always looked quite phoney to me.'

No doubt the reaction had something to do with it, for we all dissolved in laughter then. When the Commander arrived, it was quite a while before anyone could tell him just what had happened.

Written by Arthur C. Clarke
Illustrated by Gaston Vanzet

How old will I be when I get there ?

Space travel always sounds so easy in science fiction, but the truth is that the utter remoteness of our solar system from all other heavenly bodies makes any wide-ranging exploration by human beings impossible. Writers have toyed with various ideas. Put people into a state of suspended animation (i.e. a trance-like sleep during which the body does not function, therefore does not age)? But who pilots the craft? And what if you don't wake up in time and miss your destination by a hundred million kilometres or so? Or how about a group of explorers prepared to live and die on spacecraft so that their great-great-great-great-great grand kids can step out on that far distant planet? Exciting stuff for a TV series, but a few calculations soon make it seem pretty daunting. It's like imagining a First Fleeter setting out and nobody getting off the ship for 210 years until his or her 21-year-old descendent arrived in Sydney in time for the Bicentennial!

So vast is space distance, that the time it would take you to travel from one planet to another is measured in light years. Light travels at 299 792 458 kilometres per second. So in one light year you would travel approximately 9 460 528 405 000 km. (You'll never remember that, but you can still impress people by saying nonchalantly that it's around $9\frac{1}{2}$ trillion km.)

Even so, human minds still find it pretty hard to comprehend the immensity of space. Try the quiz on the next page to see how much you've picked up from all those movies and TV shows.

After you've mastered it, try out the questions on the folks at home.

Have trouble visualising where we fit in space? Try this scale.

Suppose that the Sun were reduced down to the size of a beach ball of 30 cm in diameter; if the other nine planets were also reduced according to the same scale, they would be represented *relatively* as follows:

1 Mercury = a grain of sand 15 m away.
2 Venus = a pea 24 m away
3 Earth = a pea 32 m away
 Moon = a grain of sand 8.5 cm out from the Earth
4 Mars = a currant 50 m away
5 Jupiter = an orange 171 m away
6 Saturn = a mandarin 312 m away
7 Uranus = a plum 628 m away
9 Pluto = a pinhead up to 1.6 km away
(Source: *The Guinness Book of Answers*)

It Better Be Worth the Trip! A Space Quiz

QUESTION	ANSWER
1 How long does it take for light from the most distant star in the Milky Way to reach Earth?	About 75 000 years (so the light you see tonight started out 73 000 years before Christ was born).
2 Approximately how many stars are in the Milky Way galaxy?	Around 100 000 million (Usually written as 10^{11})
3 What's our nearest star?	Centaurus. It's really a constellation of two large stars (Alpha Centauri and Beta Centauri) and a globular cluster (Omega Centauri). It's only 4.28 light years away.
4 How far is Earth from the sun?	Mean distance is 150 000 000 km (As Earth is closer at some times than others, it's necessary to work out a mean, or average, distance.)
5 How far from the sun is Pluto?	Mean distance is 5 913 000 000 km. (If you could leave from the sun and travel at the speed of light you could do the round trip in around 14 months.)
6 How far is it to Earth's nearest and furthest neighbours?	Only 40 200 000 km to Venus, but a long drag to Neptune, 4 308 000 000 km away.
7 How many galaxies are out there in the universe?	Somewhere between 100 000 and 1 000 000 million! (10^{11} to 10^{12}). Going to be hard choosing which one to visit, isn't it?
8 How big is our Milky Way galaxy?	The estimated diameter is 100 000 light years. (But that's only a tiny speck compared to radio galaxies now being discovered.)
9 Do we know anything about our neighbouring galaxies?	Yes. Astronomers have named at least 15 nearby galaxies. Most have only letters and numbers, but there's one called Sculptor and another with the name of Wolf-Lundmark. (You might like to use these in your next thrilling Sci-Fi story.)
10 How fast is Earth travelling through space?	Earth's orbital velocity (that's the average speed at which it orbits the sun) is 107 244 km/h. It's rotational velocity (that's the speed it turns on its axis) when calculated from the equator is 1674 km/h. (Better hang on tight!)

THE ORDEAL

The planet of Moros is harsh and bleak, the climate cruel, the wildlife savage. But from it comes the most superb fighting force in the Galaxy, the Legion of Moros. Its children grow up with the dream of some day becoming young legionaries and those who show high potential for advanced levels of combat training are put through a series of tests. The first, and most demanding of these, is the Ordeal.

For twelve-years-old Keill Randor, the Ordeal is proving difficult indeed. Wearing only a loin-cloth, he was left alone, unarmed and without equipment on a mountain plateau in the wilderness. His task was to find his way down through the mountains to the Colourless Valley. He has two days to reach his goal. Failure to meet up with Commander Maron will mean he has failed.

Weakened by loss of blood from a battle with a mountain wyvern (a lethal, eagle-like creature), he is desperate for food and water . . .

By late afternoon, he was feeling exactly as he had expected. Certainly the foothills now offered fewer hardships: he could follow a meandering tangle of paths through shallow vales and hollows, not needing to tackle the demanding slopes and rises. But still there was little shelter from the sun, and no sign of water among the dusty rocks and stretches of flat brown sand. The blistering fire was blazing again in his wounds. Thirst dried his mouth as if the brook in the meadow had been a dream. Hunger and weariness made his legs feel rubbery, and turned his progress into a halting plod.

So he was only dimly aware of the lengthening shadows, as the sun moved lower in the sky. And he was even less aware, as he moved along the floor of a broad, shallow gully, of the strange plants that were scattered here and there in his path.

But he became aware of them when his throbbing left arm brushed painfully against the needle-tips of thorns. He jerked away, stopping and glancing round at the cause of the new hurt. And then he might have smiled, if his lips were not cracked and crusted.

The plants had tall, spindly stems, twice Keill's height, from which trailed a number of slender growths like vines that reached to the ground and penetrated deep into the sand. These stringy growths bore the thorns — but what had stopped Keill in his tracks were the other growths, round and bulbous, that clung to the tops of the stems. Keill had seen only the domesticated sort, and then rarely, for they were hard to cultivate. But he knew what they were.

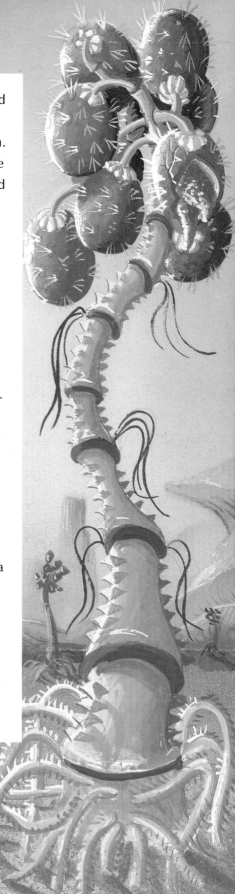

The Legions called them spikeberries, though each could be as large as a human head. They had a thick outer shell, shiny brown and bristling with their own thorny protection. But inside was a dense, moist, reddish pulp. Cooked in the Moros way, they were a delicacy. Raw, they were bitter and foul-tasting — but they were one of the few plants on Moros that humans could digest.

Reaching carefully past the thorny vines, Keill grasped the spindly stem and shook it. The spikeberries bobbled, bounced and fell, four of them, plump and bulging.

Urgently he searched for and found a narrow, flat shard of stone, and used it like a crude knifeblade to hack the fruit open. When he scooped a handful of the soggy pulp into his mouth, the mixture of feelings was almost unbearable. The pure pleasure of the wetness on his thirst-swollen tongue — but also the stomach-wrenching bitterness of the taste.

Another day he might have spat out the mouthful, gagging. But now, though he winced and shuddered, he forced himself to swallow, and to take another mouthful, and another.

Soon he was moving away through the gully, with his much-tormented loincloth now serving a new purpose, as a carrier for two spikeberries, together with the flat blade of stone. And once again he was feeling restored, as the moisture and the food poured new energy into his body.

But then he rounded a bend in the broad gully, and his hopeful thoughts were swept away like a puff of dust. The way was barred. And what was barring it was about to devote itself to the task of killing him.

Mammoths, the Legions called them. Not really as large as the name implied — no more than half again as tall as Keill. But large enough in their immense girth and ground-shaking weight. Bodies like great grey-blue boulders, with huge humped backs, six short stumpy legs. Their hide was an almost impenetrable armour, and their square, bony heads were even better armed. Wicked tusks curved up from each side of the mouth, and ridges of bone above the tiny eyes sprouted a forest of spikes and prongs, some nearly a metre long.

The mammoths moved in small herds, and ruled the foothills as the wyverns ruled the high peaks. Mammoths ate everything and anything, and had only one response to any creature foolish enough to enter their range of vision. They charged it, killed it, and ate it.

And this herd, about twenty of them, had seen Keill.

Bunched together in a solid mass of monstrous power, the mammoths charged.

Keill fled before them like a ghost. But despite their weight, their six-legged gallop was terrifyingly fast. As he sprinted up the slope, he knew they were gaining on him. And he had not even reached the crest when he realized despairingly that they were only a stride behind him.

Legion instinct made him stop and whirl, to meet death face to face. And the same instinct, or a deeply ingrained combat reflex, propelled him into a standing leap, straight up, as the lead mammoth hooked its vicious tusks up towards his belly.

He leaped, the mammoth lurched forward as its tusks found no target, and Keill came down — his feet slapping firmly on to the enormous heaving breadth of the mammoth's back. For a frozen instant he teetered there as the creature surged ahead. But balance, too, was reflexive in a legionary. As were crazy, suicidal risks — when the only alternative was certain death.

Without thinking, Keill sprang *forward*. One foot struck the boulder-like back of the mammoth just behind the leader. Instantly he found his balance, and leaped again. And so, while the herd's thunderous gallop slowed slightly as it neared the crest of the slope, Keill vaulted lightly from one immense humped back to another, across the entire herd.

It was like crossing a river on stepping stones — except that the stones themselves were moving at speed in the opposite direction, and were heaving and jolting and shifting underfoot. One small misjudgment and Keill would have been bloody pulp on the ground. But even in the choking dust thrown up by the charging beasts, Keill's eye and reactions were automatic, thought-quick and accurate as a computer. His conscious mind had only begun to catch up with what he was doing when he soared off the back of the last mammoth, fell and rolled in a flurry of dust, and sat up astonished to watch the herd disappear over the crest of the slope.

In their blind charge, the armour-hided creatures had not even noticed his leap or his weight on their backs. Their charge would probably lead them blundering on for some distance, until at last they would slow, snuffle around grumpily awhile, then wander off.

Keill stood up, trembling slightly from the exertion and delayed tension. A thought struck him. Was this, a herd of mammoths, what Commander Maron had meant, when she had spoken of 'the most deadly danger any legionary can face'? If so, he had faced it and survived it. He grinned with relief and delight at what he had done.

And the grin became an outright laugh, half-choked by the swirling dust, when he realized that he was still unthinkingly clutching his loincloth, with its precious cargo of food, in the white-knuckled grip of his right hand.

△   ◇   △   ◇   △

Hours upon hours later, the person who had laughed in the gully seemed a distant and forgotten stranger. Whatever benefit Keill had gained from the two spikeberries, much of it had been used up by the explosion of effort that had saved him from the mammoths. Even so, he had waited until full night had descended on the foothills before using his blade of stone on one of the remaining spikeberries. But this time the small amount of food and moisture was not enough to lift his energies. Fatigue was settling into the marrow of his bones, and every cell cried out for sleep.

When he came to a halt, it took several seconds for his mind to swim back to awareness, to see why he had halted. He had been stumbling along the bare and sandy bottom of yet another hollow, without noticing that the ground was sloping downwards, that the hollow was becoming deeper, narrower, turning into a canyon. But he was forced to notice, when the canyon led him to a dead end.

A sheer wall of solid earth loomed out of the blackness before him, with a heap of rock rubble at its foot. Equally steep walls rose on either side, boxing him in.

He would need to retrace his steps, which was bad enough. What was worse, he should not have been in a dead-end canyon. He was well off his route. And his exhausted mind, trying hazily to recall the map, would not produce the information he needed. He did not know where the route was. He had lost his way. He thought vaguely of eating the last spikeberry, still wrapped in the loincloth that he was clutching. But he could not muster the energy, or the interest. He let his mind slide back into its half-conscious mists sending him trudging back the way he had come like a robot.

60

When the wall of the canyon on his right became a manageable slope, it was not a conscious decision that made him wheel slowly and plod up it. Twice he stumbled and fell, once rolling several paces back down in a burst of choking dust. Each time he came to his feet more slowly than before, and plodded on.

The slope crested, and as he started down the other side he fell again, slithering down the bank of powdery sand. This time he did not rise at once. Even his automatic controls could not drag more movement from him. They were too busy trying to keep his eyelids from closing.

But slowly his eyes drooped shut. And blinked open. And closed again.

Then a muscular spasm, the sort that convulses a totally fatigued body as it sags into sleep, jolted through him, and his eyes sprang open once more. Had they closed again, he would surely have slept. And he might never have awakened, ever again.

But his eyes did not close. His blurred mind had vaguely perceived three things — which, together, shocked him awake like a spray of cold water.

First, the land around him was growing more visible. While he had been stumbling back through the canyon, the grey light of dawn had stolen into the sky.

Second, he saw that all the landscape seemed uniformly grey. But it was not only because of the dawn. It *was* grey. All the broad vista of rolling sand, featureless except for a few distant clusters of dead trees, was the same blank, empty, deathlike colour. Which was no colour at all.

The canyon where he had thought he was lost had lain only a few hundred metres from the edge of the Colourless Valley. He had reached his goal. And dawn had just broken. He might still be in time.

Except that there was the third thing he had seen, which was the most immediate and urgent shock that had spurred him into wakefulness.

No more than ten paces away, the sand was moving. Stirring, roiling, bulging upwards, as if something that had been buried was forcing its way to the surface.

And something was.

First a long, flat muzzle, the length of Keill's forearm, lifted into the air. Then a narrow head, crowned with pointed ears that swivelled like antennae. Then a slim, flexible, sinewy body, as long as Keill was tall, like a tube of powerful, lithe muscle. Head and body were covered with short, flat hair the same blank grey as the sand.

A sandcat. The most feared and lethal killer on the deserts of Moros. This creature too Keill had never seen, but he knew about it. About the razor-edges of the eight claws sprouting from each of the four broad feet. About the unbelievable speed of the thing, and its almost insane, ravening ferocity.

Sandcats were flesh eaters that also seemed to kill out of sheer blood-lust. Even the larger beasts of this region stayed clear of them, when possible. It was not always possible.

A sandcat burrowed under the sand, breathing through the tip of its muzzle, and waited for prey. Anything that passed too near would be attacked with eye-baffling speed. And those savage jaws could shear through flesh and bone as effortlessly as Keill could bite into the pulp of a spikeberry.

Keill's flesh seemed to be encased in ice. Here, of course, was what Commander Maron had meant by the deadliest danger a legionary could face. The most terrifying beast on Moros. And he was ten paces from it, naked, exhausted, totally exposed.

The sandcat became a blur as it skittered forward a pace or two. Then it halted, muzzle and ears questing. Sandcats were nearly blind, Keill knew, but their hearing and sense of smell more than compensated. Even if he did not move or breathe, it would sniff him out. Even if he had the strength to leap up and run, it would pull him down before he had taken two strides. So he lay where he was, and a dreadful empty fatalism crept over him. He had had enough.

Almost indifferently he watched the sandcat slither closer in another blurring movement, hissing softly. His face showed no emotion as he watched its muzzle and ears fix on his position — as he watched it gather itself, sinewy body poised like an arrow, the jaws parting slightly to reveal the long rows of greedy fangs.

The hiss rose into an eerie howl. Like an arrow released, jaws gaping, claws reaching, it sprang.

But in the microsecond when it was in mid-air Keill found from somewhere a last fragment of his survival instinct, a last scrap of strength. His hand clenched on the bundle that was his tattered loincloth wrapped round the one remaining spikeberry and the slim shard of rock. With that remnant of strength, he jerked his arm up — and thrust the bundle into the gaping mouth of the beast.

In the same motion he rolled desperately away. But agony exploded in his side, just above his left hip, where a razor claw sliced across his flesh. The roll brought him face down in the choking sand, where he lay feeling his blood gouting from the wound, waiting for the final agony when the sandcat recovered and found him.

But it did not come. He lifted his head, and stared with astonishment. The sandcat was threshing in a violent frenzy, only two paces away. Its mouth gaped open, and it seemed to be tearing at its own face and throat with those deadly claws.

And Keill guessed. The beast must have automatically tried to swallow what had been forced into its mouth. And, whether because of the spikeberry's tough shell or the blade of rock, the bundle had jammed in its throat. It was strangling — and dying.

But then, he thought, so am I. He looked at the terrible wound in his side, the bright red, arterial blood jetting from it. His eyes were hazy, and his muscles seemed to have turned to water. But that final vestige of his instinct to survive brought his hand down and clamped it over the wound, compressing its edges together.

After moments that seemed like days, he struggled with infinite slowness to his feet, his hand automatically maintaining the fierce pressure on his wound.

Behind him, the sandcat's death throes subsided into stillness. But he hardly noticed. Nor was he really aware — except in the deepest core of his being, where those last shreds of his instincts lay — that he had begun to walk, swaying, staggering, but moving forward.

Twenty minutes later he was no longer walking. But he was still moving — on his knees and one hand, the other hand still relentlessly clamped on his dripping wound. By then he was nearly unconscious. He did not hear the rapid footsteps in the sand. He did not hear the gasp, and the muttered exclamation. But he felt the hands that grasped him and began to lift him up. And the vague movements he made might even have been a struggle.

"Keill, you've arrived," said a quiet voice. "Stop now. It's over."

No one could ever be sure, afterwards, whether he collapsed into unconsciousness merely *as* those words were spoken — or because of them.

Later Keill learns that the deadliest danger during the Ordeal was not the journey through the harsh terrain or the ferocious creatures that inhabited the wilderness. It was simply fear — the kind of fear that weakened the will, preventing him from going on, even in the face of impossible odds.

Written by Douglas Hill
Illustrated by Peter Schmidli

MENTAL FITNESS

Most of us carry a lot of "mind garbage" around with us — all those fears, worries and imaginary problems. Learning how to dump them could be the best skill you'll acquire this year. Remember: "There's nothing to fear but fear itself".

> Goodbye and good riddance to bad rubbish.

MIND GARBAGE

— video nasties
— horror movies
— fights with a friend
— jealous thoughts
— gloom and doom
— real things that scare, e.g. mean dogs
— hate and gossip
— worries about things that *might* happen (but usually don't).

HOW TO DUMP GARBAGE

A. Order scary thoughts to "Go in peace".

B. Make a list of all your mistakes or fears then screw it up and burn it in a safe place.

C. Imagine you're putting all the garbage in a big sack and dumping if off the side of a ship or burying it.

1 Clean the windows of your mind. Then you'll be able to see things clearly.

2 When all the dumping and cleaning has been done and your mind's quite empty, fill it up again with quiet, pleasant thoughts.

3 Concentrate on developing a strong, healthy body and a strong, healthy mind.

> Ah! Much better!

> Yippeee!

HOW TO PREVENT GARBAGE ACCUMULATING

1 Imagine you're surrounded by a beautiful circle of shimmering white light. The light protects you.

2 Think positively. Look for the good things that happen to you, no matter how small.

3 Find a quiet spot where you can sit and be alone for ten minutes, especially if you're not feeling good. Shut your eyes and imagine you're sitting in a beautiful, peaceful place. Try this daily.

4 Every night in bed, take a deep breath in and as you slowly breathe out, imagine all your problems floating away. Look forward to the morning.

5 Become like the three wise monkeys and choose to see no evil, hear no evil and speak no evil.

6 Last but not least, take a feather from Ozzie Ostrich's notebook and simply bury your head in the sand. (As long as it's not an excuse for refusing to face up to life!)

Margarette Thomas-Cochran

DANIEL

INSCRIBED TO ISADOR BENNETT REED

(a poem to chant, sing — or just ham up a bit!)

Beginning with a strain of 'Dixie'

Darius the Mede was a king and a wonder.
His eye was proud, and his voice was thunder.
He kept bad lions in a monstrous den.
He fed up the lions on Christian men.

With a touch of Alexander's Ragtime Band'

Daniel was the chief hired man of the land.
He stirred up the music in the palace band.
He whitewashed the cellar. He shovelled in the coal.
And Daniel kept a-praying: "Lord save my soul."
Daniel kept a-praying: "Lord save my soul."
Daniel kept a-praying: "Lord save my soul."

Daniel was the butler, swagger and swell.
He ran up stairs. He answered the bell.
And *he* would let in whoever came a-calling:
Saints so holy, scamps so appalling.
"Old man Ahab leaves his card.
Elisha and the bears are a-waiting in the yard.
Here comes Pharaoh and his snakes a-calling.
Here comes Cain and his wife a-calling.
Shadrach, Meshach and Abednego for tea.
Here comes Jonah and the whale,
And the *Sea*!
Here comes St Peter and his fishing pole.
Here comes Judas and his silver a-calling.
here comes old Beelzebub a -calling."
And Daniel kept a-praying: "Lord save my soul."
Daniel kept a-praying: "Lord save my soul."
Daniel kept a-praying: "Lord save my soul."

His sweetheart and his mother were Christian and meek.
They washed and ironed for Darius every week.
One Thursday he met them at the door:
Paid them as usual, but acted sore.

He said: "Your Daniel is a dead little pigeon.
He's a good hard worker, but he talks religion."
And he showed them Daniel in the lion's cage.
Daniel standing quietly, the lions in a rage.
His good old mother cried:
"Lord save him."
And Daniel's tender sweetheart cried:
"Lord save him."

This to be repeated
three times, very
softly and slowly
And she was a golden lily in the dew.
And she was as sweet as an apple on the tree
And she was as fine as a melon in the corn-field,
Gliding and lovely as a ship on the sea,
Gliding and lovely as a ship on the sea.

And she prayed to the Lord:
"Send Gabriel. Send Gabriel."

King Darius said to the lions:
"Bite Daniel. Bite Daniel.
Bite him. Bite him. Bite him!"

Here the audience
roars with the
leader
Thus roared the lions:
"We want Daniel, Daniel, Daniel.
We want Daniel, Daniel, Daniel.
Grrrrrrrrrrrrrrrrrrrrrrrrrrrrrrrrrrrrrrrrrr
Grrrrrrrrrrrrrrrrrrrrrrrrrrrrrrrrrrrrrrrrrrrrr."

And Daniel did not frown.
Daniel did not cry.
He kept on looking at the sky.
And the Lord said to Gabriel:
"Go chain the lions down,
The audience
sings this with the
leader, to the old
Afro/Caribbean tune
Go chain the lions down.
Go chain the lions down.
Go chain the lions down."

And Gabriel chained the lions,
And Gabriel chained the lions,
And Gabriel chained the lions,

And Daniel got out of the den,
And Daniel got out of the den,
And Daniel got out of the den,
And Darius said: "You're a Christian child,"
Darius said: "You're a Christian child,"
Darius said: "You're a Christian child."
And gave him his job again.
And gave him his job again.
And gave him his job again.

Vachel Lindsay

WHY TILT AT WINDMILLS ?

Meet Don Quixote the nuttiest knight you could imagine. He's so simple-minded that he mistakes a windmill for a giant and actually challenges it to battle.

Where does he come from?

He's the hero of a famous novel by the Spanish writer, Miguel de Cervantes Saavedra who lived from 1547 to 1616. Cervantes, as he's usually called, didn't begin writing until later life. He was a fairly adventurous fellow who went off to Italy in search of work and ended up enlisting as a sailor in a naval expedition that the King of Spain, the Pope and the Venetian officials were preparing to send against the Turks. He was soon put to the test, for he went out to fight even though he was sick with a high fever. But his bravery didn't stop him being wounded, and in the battle his left arm and hand were badly damaged. He could never use them again.

This was in 1571. Four years later Cervantes decided to return to Spain, hoping the King might reward him in some way. But fate was against him. His ship was hijacked by a bunch of Turkish pirates and he was taken to Algiers and held hostage. Five long years passed before Cervantes' family managed to raise the ransom and by then it seems, no one was interested in a crippled returned soldier. He took a job collecting grain and olive oil for the Spanish Armada that King Philip was busy organising, but landed in jail, accused of having his hand in the till. It's believed that he probably began to write about Don Quixote while imprisoned.

So what makes Don Quixote special?

The Don Quixote that Cervantes invented was a country gentleman from La Mancha in central Spain. He's gentle, dignified, affectionate — and just a little simple-minded. He's been reading romantic stories about knights and their chivalry and he's convinced himself they are all true. He decides to become a knight and go out and right all the wrongs in his personal world.

He rummages around in the ancestral home and finds himself some battered old bits of armour that used to belong to his great grandfather. He dresses himself up, making a visor for the helmet out of paper and cardboard. Then he dusts off two or three weapons that were rusting on the wall and finds himself a horse. She's an equally battered skin-and-bones old animal, but Don Quixote thinks her perfect. Before long he also acquires a squire, a not-very-bright fellow called Sancho Panza. Sancho is short, pot-bellied (*panza* means "paunch" in Spanish) and very gullible. He believes everything Don Quixote tells him, especially the fact that he, Sancho, will be made governor of an island.

So they begin their adventures. Few turn out the way Don Quixote expects for he imagines he's living in a world quite different from the real one. For him, inns are castles, ordinary working women and men are lords and ladies, and windmills are giants. Everyone plays along with him (more or less), thinking him mad, though a few "maidens in distress" rescued against their will get pretty irritable. Finally poor Don Quixote realises that the stories were just pure fiction and recovers his wits — just before he dies.

Why should he be remembered?

Don Quixote's name has been turned into a word. A quixotic person is a romantic dreamer, one whose ideas about honour or doing good couldn't possibly work.

Another phrase from the book is "to tilt at windmills". To tilt meant thrusting with a lance, the long weapon used by knights in battle. When you say a person is tilting at windmills, it means he or she is wasting energy facing up to imaginary enemies, is fighting something that doesn't exist. It's no test of courage at all.

Long ago there ruled a great king in Athens called Aegeus, and his son, Theseus, was a hero who had done many brave and mighty deeds.

Now the whole country was happy and at peace except for one great sorrow. Minos, king of Crete, had fought against the Athenians and had conquered them; and before returning to Crete he had made a hard and cruel peace. Each year the Athenians were forced to send seven young men and seven maidens to be sacrificed to the Minotaur. This was a monster who lived in the labyrinth, a winding path among rocks and caves. So each spring seven youths and maidens, chosen by lot, journeyed in a ship with black sails to the shores of Crete, to be torn to pieces by the savage Minotaur.

One spring, when the herald from King Minos arrived, Theseus determined to make an end of the beast and rid his father's people of this horrible evil. He went and told Aegeus that when the black-sailed ship set out on the morrow he would go too and slay the Minotaur.

"But how will you slay him, my son?" said Aegeus. "For you must leave your club and your shield behind, and be cast to the monster, defenceless and naked like the rest."

And Theseus said, "Are there no stones in that labyrinth; and have I not fists and teeth?"

Then Aegeus clung to his knees; but he would not hear; and at last he let him go, weeping bitterly, and said only this one word:

romise me but this, if you return in peace, though that may hardly be, take down the black sail of the ship (for I shall watch for it all day upon the cliffs), and hoist instead a white sail, that I may know afar off that you are safe."

And Theseus promised, and went out, and to the market-place where the herald stood, while they drew lots for the youths and maidens, who were to sail in that doleful crew. And the people stood wailing and weeping, as the lot fell on this one and on that; but Theseus strode into the midst, and cried:

"Here is a youth who needs no lot. I myself will be one of the seven."

And the herald asked in wonder, "Fair youth, know you whither you are going?"

And Theseus said, "I know. Let us go down to the black-sailed ship."

So they went down to the black-sailed ship, seven maidens and seven youths, and Theseus before them all, and the people following them lamenting. But Theseus whispered to his companions, "Have hope, for the monster is not immortal." Then their hearts were comforted a little; but they wept as they went on board, and the cliffs of Sunium rang, and all the isles of the Aegean Sea, with the voice of their lamentation, as they sailed on towards their deaths in Crete.

And at last they came to Crete, and to Cnossus, beneath the peaks of Ida, and to the palace of Minos the great king, to whom Zeus himself taught laws. So he was the wisest of all mortal kings, and conquered all the Aegean isles; and his ships were as many as the sea-gulls, and his palace like a marble hill.

ut Theseus stood before Minos, and they looked each other in the face. And Minos bade take them to prison, and cast them to the monster one by one. Then Theseus cried:

"A boon, O Minos! Let me be thrown first to the beast. For I came hither for that very purpose, of my own will, and not by lot."

"Who art thou, then, brave youth?"

"I am the son of him whom of all men thou hatest most, Aegeus, the king of Athens, and I am come here to end this matter."

And Minos pondered awhile, looking steadfastly at him, and he answered at last mildly:

"Go back in peace, my son. It is a pity that one so brave should die."

But Theseus said, "I have sworn that I will not go back till I have seen the monster face to face."

And at that Minos frowned, and said, "Then thou shalt see him; take the madman away."

And they led Theseus away into prison, with the other youths and maids.

But Ariadne, Minos' daughter, saw him as she came out of her white stone hall; and she loved him for his courage and his majesty, and said, "Shame that such a youth should die!" And by night she went down to the prison, and told him all her heart, and said:

"Flee down to your ship at once, for I have bribed the guards before the door. Flee, you and all your friends, and go back in peace to Greece; and take me, take me with you! for I dare not stay after you are gone; for my father will kill me miserably, if he knows what I have done."

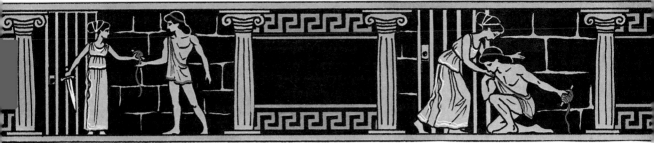

nd Theseus stood silent awhile; for he was astonished and confounded by her beauty; but at last he said, "I cannot go home in peace till I have seen and slain this Minotaur, and avenged the deaths of the youths and maidens, and put an end to the terrors of my land."

"And will you kill the Minotaur? How, then?"

"I know not, nor do I care; but he must be strong if he be too strong for me."

Then she loved him all the more, and said, "But when you have killed him, how will you find your way out of the labyrinth?"

"I know not, neither do I care; but it must be a strange road, if I do not find it out before I have eaten up the monster's carcase."

Then she loved him all the more, and said:

"Fair youth, you are too bold; but I can help you, weak as I am. I will give you a sword, and with that perhaps you may slay the beast; and a clue of thread, and by that, perhaps, you may find your way out again. Only promise me that if you escape safe you will take me home with you to Greece; for my father will surely kill me, if he knows what I have done."

Then Theseus laughed and said, "Am I not safe enough now?" And he hid the sword in his bosom, and rolled up the clue in his hand; and then he swore to Ariadne, and fell down before her and kissed her hands and her feet; and she wept over him a long while, and then went away; and Theseus lay down and slept sweetly.

When the evening came, the guards came in and led him away to the labyrinth.

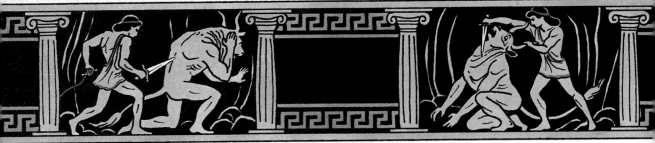

nd he went down into that doleful gulf, through winding paths among the rocks, under caverns, and arches, and galleries, and over heaps of fallen stone. And he turned on the left hand, and on the right hand, and went up and down, till his head was dizzy; but all the while he held his clue. For when he went in he had fastened it to a stone, and left it to unroll out of his hand as he went on; and it lasted him till he met the Minotaur, in a narrow chasm between black cliffs.

And when he saw him he stopped awhile, for he had never seen so strange a beast. His body was a man's; but his head was the head of a bull, and his teeth were the teeth of a lion, and with them he tore his prey. And when he saw Theseus he roared, and put his head down, and rushed right at him.

But Theseus stept aside nimbly, and as he passed by, cut him in the knee; and ere he could turn in the narrow path, he followed him, and stabbed him again and again from behind, till the monster fled bellowing wildly; for he never before had felt a wound. And Theseus followed him at full speed, holding the clue of thread in his left hand.

Then on, through cavern after cavern, under dark ribs of sounding stone, and up rough glens and torrent-beds, among the sunless roots of Ida, and to the edge of the eternal snow, went they, the hunter and the hunted, while the hills bellowed to the monster's bellow.

And at last Theseus came up with him, where he lay panting on a slab among the snows, and caught him by the horns, and forced his head back, and drove the keen sword through his throat.

hen he turned, and went back limping and weary, feeling his way down by the clue of thread till he came to the mouth of that doleful place; and saw waiting for him, whom but Ariadne!

And he whispered, "It is done" and showed her the sword; and she laid her finger on her lips and led him to the prison, and opened the doors, and set all the prisoners free, while the guards lay sleeping heavily; for she had silenced them with wine.

Then they fled to their ship together, and leapt on board, and hoisted up the sail; and the night lay dark around them, so that they passed through Minos' ships, and escaped all safe to Naxos; and there Ariadne became Theseus' wife.

But that fair Ariadne never came to Athens with her husband. Some say that Theseus left her sleeping on Naxos among the Cyclades; and that Dionysus the wine-king found her, and took her up into the sky. And some say that Dionysus drove away Theseus, and took Ariadne from him by force; but however that may be, in his haste or in his grief, Theseus forgot to put up the white sail. Now Aegeus his father sat and watched on Sunium day after day, and strained his old eyes across the sea to see the ship afar. And when he saw the black sail, and not the white one, he gave up Theseus for dead, and in his grief he fell into the sea, and died; so it is called Aegean to this day.

And now Theseus was king of Athens, and he guarded it and ruled it well.

Written by Charles Kingsley

Illustrated by Elizabeth Alger

The Playground

Just where the river curled out to meet the sea was the town playground, and next to the playground in a tall cream-coloured house lived Linnet. Every day after school she stood for a while at her window watching the children over the fence, and longing to run out and join them. She could hear the squeak squeak of the swings going up and down, up and down all afternoon. She could see children bending their knees pushing themselves up into the sky. She would think to herself, "Yes, I'll go down now. I won't stop to think about it. I'll run out and have a turn on the slide," but then she would feel her hands getting hot and her stomach shivery, and she knew she was frightened again.

Jim her brother and Alison her sister (who was a year younger than Linnet) were not frightened of the playground. Alison could fly down the slide with her arms held wide, chuckling as she went. Jim would spin on the roundabout until he felt more like a top than a boy, then he would jump off and roll over in the grass shouting with laughter. But when Linnet went on the slide the smooth shiny wood burned the backs of her legs, and she shot off the end so fast she tumbled over and made all the other children laugh. When she went on the roundabout the trees and the sky smudged into one another and she felt sick. Even the swings frightened her and she held their chains so tightly that the links left red marks in her hands.

"Why should I be so scared?" she wondered. "If only I could get onto the swing and swing without thinking about it I'd be all right. Only babies fall off. I wouldn't mind being frightened of lions or wolves but it is terrible to be frightened of swings and seesaws."

Then a strange thing happened. Linnet's mother forgot to pull the blind down one night. The window was open and a little wind came in smelling of the ropes and tar on the wharf and of the salt sea beyond. Linnet sighed in her sleep and turned over. Then the moon began to set lower in the sky. It found her window and looked in at her. Linnet woke up.

The moonlight made everything quite different and
enchanted. The river was pale and smooth and its other
bank, the sandspit around which it twisted to find the sea,
was absolutely black. The playground which was so noisy
and crowded by day was deserted. It looked strange
because it was so still and because the red roundabout, the
green slide, and the blue swings were all grey in the
moonlight. It looked like the ghost of a playground, or a
faded clockwork toy waiting for daylight, and happy
children to wind it up and set it going again. Linnet heard
the town clock strike faintly. Midnight. She thought some
of the moon silver must have got into the clock's works
because it sounded softer, yet clearer than it did during the
day. As she thought this she was startled to see shadows
flicker over the face of the moon. "Witches?" she
wondered before she had time to tell herself that witches
were only make-believe people. Of course it wasn't witches.
It was a flock of birds flying inland from the sea.

"They're going to land on the river bank," she thought.
"How funny, I didn't know birds could fly at night. I
suppose it is because it is such bright moonlight."

They landed and were lost to sight in a moment, but just as she began to look somewhere else a new movement caught her eye and she looked back again. Out from under the trees fringing the riverbank, from the very place where the birds had landed, came children running, bouncing and tumbling: their voices and laughter came to her, faint as chiming clock bells.

Linnet could see their bare feet shaking and crushing the grass, their wild floating hair, and even their mischievous shining eyes. They swarmed all over the playground. The swings began to swing, the seesaws started their up and down, the roundabout began to spin. The children laughed and played and frolicked while Linnet watched them, longing more than ever before to run out and join in the fun. It wasn't that she was afraid of the playground this time — it was just that she was shy. So she had to be content to stare while all the time the swings swept back and forth loaded with the midnight children, and still more children crowded the roundabout, the seesaw and the bars.

How long she watched
Linnet could not say. She fell
asleep watching, and woke up
with her cheek on the window-
sill. The morning playground
was quite empty and was
bright in its daytime colours
once more.

"Was it all dreams?" wondered Linnet blinking over
breakfast. "Will they come again tonight?"

"Wake up, stupid," Alison called. "It's time to be off.
We'll be late for school."

All day Linnet wondered about the playground and the
children playing there by moonlight. She seemed slower
and quieter than ever. Jim and Alison teased her calling
her Old Dreamy, but Linnet did not tell them what dreams
she had.

84

That night the moon woke Linnet once more and she sat
up in a flash, peering out anxiously to see if the midnight
children were there. The playground, colourless and strange
in its nightdress, was empty, but within a minute Linnet
heard the beat of wings in the night. Yes, there were the
birds coming in from the sea, landing under the trees and,
almost at once, there were the children, moonlit and
laughing, running to the playground for their night games.
Linnet leaned farther out of her window to watch them,
and one of them suddenly saw her and pointed at her. All
the children came and stood staring over the fence at her.
For a few seconds they just stayed like that, Linnet peering
out at them and the midnight children, moon-silver and
smiling, looking back at her. Their hair, blown behind them
by the wind, was as pale as sea foam. Their eyes were as
dark and deep as sea caves and shone like stars.

Then the children began to beckon and wave and jump
up and down with their arms half out to her, they began to
skip and dance with delight. Linnet slid out of bed, climbed
out of the window and over the fence all in her nightgown.
The midnight children crowded up to her, caught her and
whirled her away.

Linnet thought it was like dancing some strange dance.
At one moment she was on the roundabout going round
and round and giggling with the other children at the
prickly dizzy feeling it gave her, in the next she was
sweeping in a follow-my-leader down the slide. Then
someone took her hand and she was on the seesaw with a
child before her and a child behind and three more on the
other end.

Up went the seesaw.

"Oh, I'm flying!" cried Linnet. Down went the seesaw.
Bump went Linnet, and she laughed at the unexpected
bouncy jolt when the seesaw end hit the rubber tyre
beneath it. Then she was on the swing. She had never been
so high before. It seemed to Linnet that at any moment the
swing was going to break free and fly off on its own,
maybe to the land where the midnight children came from.
The swing felt like a great black horse plunging through the
night, like a tall ship tossing over the green waves.

"Oh," cried Linnet, "it's like having wings." The children laughed with her, waved and smiled, and they swept around in their playground dance, but they didn't speak. Sometimes she heard them singing, but they were always too far away for her to hear the words.

When, suddenly, the midnight children left their games and started to run for the shadow of the trees, Linnet knew that for tonight at least she must go home as well, but she was too excited to feel sad. As she climbed through the window again she heard the beat of wings in the air and saw the birds flying back to the sea. She waved to them, but in the next moment they were quite gone, and she and the playground were alone again.

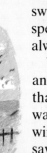

Next day when Alison and Jim set out for the playground Linnet said she was coming too. "Don't come to me if you fall off anything," said Jim scornfully.

Alison was kinder. "I'll help you on the roundabout," she said. "You hang on to me if you feel giddy."

"But I won't feel giddy!" Linnet said, and Alison stared at her, surprised to hear her so confident and happy. However, this was just the beginning of the surprises for Alison and Jim. Linnet went on the roundabout and sat there without hanging on at all. On the swing she went almost as high as the boys, and she sat on the seesaw with her arms folded.

"Gosh, Linnet's getting brave as anything over at the playground," said Jim at tea that night.

86   "I always knew she had it in her," said Daddy.

The next night, and the next, Linnet climbed out of her window and joined the beckoning children in the silver playground. During the day, these midnight hours seemed like enchanted dreams and not very real. All the same Linnet was happy and excited knowing she had a special secret all to herself. Her eyes sparkled, she laughed a lot, and got braver and braver in the playground until all the children stopped what they were doing to watch her.

"Gee, Mum," Alison said, "you should see Linnet. She goes higher on the swing than any of the boys — much higher than Jim. Right up almost over the top."

"I hope you're careful, dear," her mother said.

"I'm all right," Linnet cried. "I'm not the least bit scared."

"Linnet used to be frightened as anything," Alison said, "but now she's braver than anybody else."

Linnet's heart swelled with pride. She could hardly wait until the moon and the tide brought her wonderful laughing night-time companions. She wanted them to admire her and gasp at her as the other children did. They came as they had on other nights, and she scrambled over the fence to join them.

"Look at me!" she shouted, standing on the end of the seesaw and going up and down. The child on the other end laughed and stood up too, but on its hands, not on its feet. It stayed there not over-balancing at all. Linnet slid away as soon as she could and ran over to the swings. She worked herself up higher and higher until she thought she was lost among the stars far far above the playground and the world, all on her own.

"Look at me," she called again. "Look at me."

But the child on the next swing smiled over its shoulder and went higher — just a little higher. Then Linnet lost her temper.

"It's cleverer for me," she shouted, "because I'm a real live child, but you — you're only a flock of birds."

Suddenly silence fell, the laughter died away, the singers stopped their songs. The swings swung lower, the roundabout turned slower, the seesaws stopped for a moment. Linnet saw all the children's pale faces turn towards her: then, without a sound, they began to run back to the shadow of the trees. Linnet felt cold with sadness. "Don't go," she called. "Please don't go." They did not seem to hear her.

"I'm sorry I said it," she cried after them, her voice sounding very small and thin in the moonlit silent playground. "I didn't mean it." But no — they would not stop even though she pleaded, "Don't go!" yet again. The playground was empty already and she knew she couldn't follow her midnight children. For the last time she spoke to them.

"I'm sorry!" she whispered and, although it was only a whisper, they must have heard because they answered her. Their voices and laughter drifted back happy and friendly saying their own goodbye. The next moment she saw for the last time the birds flying back over the sea to the secret land they came from. Linnet stood alone and barefooted in the playground, the wind pulling at her nightgown. How still and empty it was now. She pushed at a swing and it moved giving a sad little squeak that echoed all round. There was nothing for Linnet to do but go back to bed.

She was never afraid of the playground again and had lots and lots of happy days there laughing and chattering with her friends. Yet sometimes at night, when the moon rose and looked in at her window, she would wake up and look out at the playground just in case she should see the moon and the tide bringing her a flock of strange night-flying birds, which would turn into children and call her out to play with them. But the playground was always empty, the shining midnight children, with their songs and laughter, were gone forever.

Written by Margaret Mahy
Illustrated by Judy Byford

SCOTLAND

Scotland is a country of great beauty, with many lochs (lakes), high mountains and a very varied sea coast. The eastern side of Scotland has a relatively straight coastline. On the western side, however, the coastline is extremely indented, and there are many islands — the Inner and Outer Hebrides.

Although it is part of Great Britain, Scotland has its own legal, educational and ecclesiastical systems. Banks issue their own bank notes (including pound notes, although these aren't used in England anymore) and postage stamps carry the Scottish lion.

19ᴾ

The capital of Scotland is Edinburgh, although Glasgow is in fact the bigger city. Both are historic cities that are now important cultural and business centres. Edinburgh hosts an international arts festival every summer in August. Glasgow has many varied cultural events and attractions: in 1988 it held a Garden Festival for five months over the summer as well as a Jazz Festival. It was chosen as European City of Culture for 1990. Other important cities in Scotland include Aberdeen and Dundee on the north-east coast, and Inverness which is the largest Highland town.

Edinburgh

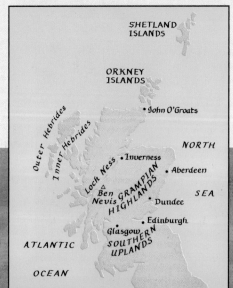

Glasgow

Traditionally Scottish men wear kilts which are pleated skirts made from Tartan (checked woollen) material. In front of the kilt they wear a sporran: a pouch made from animal skin. This Scotsman is playing the bagpipes — an instrument with several pipes that are played simultaneously. There is a 'melody' pipe, and three 'drone' pipes, which play continuous low notes. The drone pipes are thrown over the left shoulder, and the bag storing the air to play the drone pipes is held under the arm.

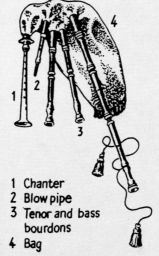

1 Chanter
2 Blow pipe
3 Tenor and bass bourdons
4 Bag

Although other lochs are longer, deeper or with a larger surface area, Loch Ness is the biggest loch in that it holds the most water. It is famous for the monster said to live in its depths. There have been many reported sightings of the Loch Ness monster and photographs of various kinds, but even using modern sonar equipment nothing conclusive has yet been found.

Gilly Shows Them!

Eleven-year-old Gilly Hopkin's life has been one foster home after another. If there is a single lesson she has learned it is that you have to be tough to survive — super tough and super cool. The more she can bug the adults in her life with her anti-social behaviour, the better she feels, believing somehow that if the mother who had abandoned her hears of her problems, she will come and claim her. Now Gilly is in her third home in less than three years. This one belongs to big, fat, Bible-quoting Maime Trotter who is also caring for a little black boy named William Ernest whom Gilly delights in terrorising.

With her first day ahead at yet another new school, Gilly sets out to be as provocative as possible . . .

In the tiny mirror over the bureau Gilly noted with no little satisfaction that her hair was a wreck. Yesterday before the bubble gum got into it, it had looked as though it simply needed combing. Today it looked like a lot that had been partially bulldozed — an uprooted tree here, a half wall with a crumbling chimney there. It was magnificent. It would run Trotter wild. Gilly bounced down the stairs and into the kitchen.

She held her head very straight as she sat at the kitchen table and waited for the fireworks.

"I'll take you down to the school a little after nine, hear?" Trotter said.

Of course Gilly heard. She tilted her head a little in case Trotter couldn't *see.*

"If I take you down earlier," Trotter went on, "we'll just have to sit and wait till they can take care of us. I'd as leave sit here at my own table with a cup of coffee, wouldn't you?" She put a bowl of steaming hot cereal down in front of Gilly.

Gilly nodded her head vigorously Yes.

William Ernest was staring at her, his glasses steamed up from the oatmeal. Gilly bared her teeth and shook her head violently No at him. The boy snuffled loudly and ducked his head.

"Need a tissue, William Ernest?" Trotter pulled one from her apron pocket and gently wiped his nose. "And here's a clean one for school, honey." Trotter leaned over and tucked a tissue into his pants pocket.

Gilly craned her neck over the table as though she were trying to see the contents of W.E.'s pocket. Her head was within a couple of feet of Trotter's eyes. The woman was sure to notice.

"William Ernest got promoted to the Orange reading group yesterday. Didn't you, William Ernest, honey?"

The little boy nodded his head but kept his eyes on his bowl.

"You're gonna have to do some reading out loud and show Gilly how great you're coming along with your reading these days."

W.E. looked up for one split second with terror in his eyes. Trotter missed the look, but not Gilly, who smiled widely and shook her half-bulldozed head emphatically. "In Orange they use hardback books," Trotter was explaining. "It's a real big step to be Orange." She leaned over Gilly to put some toast on the table. "We really worked for this."

"So old W.E.'s getting a *head*, is he?"

Trotter gave her a puzzled look. "Yeah, he's doing just fine."

"Before you know it," Gilly heard herself saying loudly, "he'll be blowing his own nose and *combing his own hair*."

"He already does,' said Trotter quietly. "Leastways most of the time." She sat down with a loud sigh at the table. "Pass me a piece of toast, will you, Gilly?"

93

Gilly picked up the plate, raised it to the height of her hair, and passed it across to Trotter at that level.

"Thank you, honey."

At eight thirty Trotter got William Ernest off to school. Gilly had long since finished her breakfast, but she sat at the kitchen table, her head propped on her fists. From the doorway she could hear Old Mother Goose honking over her gosling. "OK, Big Orange, you show 'em down there today, hear?" Trotter said finally; and then the heavy door shut and she was heading back for the kitchen. As she got to the door, Gilly sat up straight and shook her head for all she was worth.

"You got a tic or something, honey?"

"No."

"I would've thought you was too young for the palsy," the huge woman murmured, sliding into her seat with the cup of coffee she'd promised herself earlier. "I see you got sneakers. That's good. You're supposed to have them for gym. Can you think of anything else you'll need for school?"

Gilly shook her head, but halfheartedly. She was beginning to feel like an oversharpened pencil.

"I think I'll go upstairs till it's time," she said.

"Oh, while you're up there, honey —"

"Yeah?" Gilly sprang to attention.

"Make the beds, will you? It does look messy to leave 'em unmade all day, and I'm not much on running up and down the stairs."

Gilly banged the door to her room for all she was worth. She spit every obscenity she'd ever heard through her teeth, but it wasn't enough. That ignorant hippopotamus! That walrus-faced imbecile! That — that — oh, the devil — Trotter wouldn't even let a drop fall from her precious William Ernest baby's nose, but she would let Gilly go to school — a new school where she didn't know anybody — looking like a scarecrow. Miss Ellis would surely hear about this. Gilly slammed her fist into her pillow. There had to be a law against foster mothers who showed such gross favouritism.

Well, she would show that lard can a thing or two. She yanked open the left top drawer, pulling out a broken comb, which she viciously jerked through the wilderness on her head, only to be defeated by a patch of bubble gum. She ran into the bathroom and rummaged through the medicine chest until she found a pair of nail scissors with which to chop out the offending hair. When despite her assault by comb and scissors a few strands refused to lie down meekly, she soaked them mercilessly into submission. She'd show the world. She'd show them who Galadriel Hopkins was — she was not to be trifled with.

"I see they call you Gilly," said Mr Evans, the principal.

"I can't even pronounce the poor child's real name," said Trotter, chuckling in what she must believe was a friendly manner.

It didn't help Gilly's mood. She was still seething over the hair combing.

"Well, Gilly's a fine name," said Mr Evans, which confirmed to Gilly that at school, too, she was fated to be surrounded by fools.

The principal was studying records that must have been sent over from Gilly' former school, Hollywood Gardens Elementary. He coughed several times. "Well," he said, "I think this young lady needs to be in a class that will challenge her."

"She's plenty smart, if that's what you mean."

Trotter, you dummy. How do you know how smart I am? You never laid eyes on me until yesterday.

"I'm going to put you into Miss Harris's class. We have some departmentalization in the sixth grade, but . . ."

"You got *what* in the sixth grade?"

Oh, Trotter, shut your fool mouth.

But the principal didn't seem to notice what a dope Trotter was. He explained patiently how some of the sixth-grade classes moved around for math and reading and science, but Miss Harris kept the same group all day.

What a blinking bore.

They went up three flights of ancient stairway to Miss Harris's room slowly, so that Trotter would not collapse. The corridors stank of oiled floors and cafeteria soup. Gilly had thought she hated all schools so much that they no longer could pain or disappoint her, but she felt heavier with each step — like a condemned prisoner walking an endless last mile.

They paused before the door marked "Harris — 6". Mr Evans knocked, and a tall tea-coloured woman, crowned with a bush of black hair, opened the door. She smiled down on the three of them, because she was even taller than the principal.

Gilly shrank back, bumping into Trotter's huge breast, which made her jump forward again quickly. God, on top of everything else, the teacher was black.

No one seemed to take notice of her reaction, unless you counted a flash of brightness in Miss Harris's dark eyes.

Trotter patted Gilly's arm, murmured something that ended in "honey", and then she and the principal floated backward, closing Gilly into Harris — 6. The teacher led her to an empty desk in the middle of the classroom, asked for Gilly's jacket, which she handed over to another girl to hang on the coatrack at the back of the room. She directed Gilly to sit down, and then went up and settled herself at the large teacher's desk to glance through the handful of papers Mr Evans had given her.

In a moment she looked up, a warm smile lighting her face. "Galadriel Hopkins. What a beautiful name! From Tolkien, of course."

"No," muttered Gilly. "Hollywood Gardens."

Miss Harris laughed a sort of golden laugh. "No, I mean your name — Galadriel. It's the name of a great queen in a book by a man named Tolkien. But, of course, you know that."

Hell. No one had ever told her that her name came from a book. Should she pretend she knew all about it or play dumb?

"I'd like to call you Galadriel, if you don't mind. It's such a lovely name."

"No!" Everyone was looking at Gilly peculiarly. She must have yelled louder than she intended to. "I would prefer," she said tightly, "to be called Gilly."

"Yes" — Miss Harris's voice was more steel than gold now — "Yes. Gilly, it is then. Well" — she turned her smile on the rest of the class — "Where were we?"

The clamour of their answers clashed in Gilly's brain. She started to put her head down on the desk, but someone was shoving a book into her face.

It wasn't fair — nothing was fair. She had once seen a picture in an old book of a red fox on a high rock surrounded by snarling dogs. It was like that. She was smarter than all of them, but they were too many. They had her surrounded, and in their stupid ways, they were determined to wear her down.

Miss Harris was leaning over her. Gilly pulled away as far as she could.

"Did you do division with fractions at Hollywood Gardens?"

Gilly shook her head. Inside she seethed. It was bad enough having to come to this broken-down old school but to be behind — to seem dumber than the rest of the kids — to have to appear a fool in front of . . . Almost half the class was black. And she would look dumb to *them*. A bunch of —

"Why don't you bring your chair up to my desk, and we'll work on it?"

Gilly snatched up her chair and beat Miss Harris to the front of the room. She'd show them!

At recesstime Monica Bradley, one of the other white girls in the class, was supposed to look after her on the playground. But Monica was more interested in leaning against the building and talking with her friends, which she did, keeping her back toward Gilly as she giggled and gossiped with two other sixth-grade girls, one of whom was black with milions of tiny braids all over her head. Like some African bushwoman. Not that Gilly cared. Why should she? They could giggle their stupid lives away, and she'd never let it bother her. She turned her back on them. That would show them.

Just then a ball jerked loose from the basketball game nearby and rushed toward her. She grabbed it. Balls were friends. She hugged it and ran over to the basket and threw it up, but she had been in too much of a hurry. It kissed the rim but refused to go in for her. Angrily she jumped and caught it before it bounced. She was dimly aware of a protest from the players, but they were boys and mostly shorter than she, so not worthy of notice. She shot again, this time with care. It arched and sank cleanly. She pushed someone out of the way and grabbed it just below the net.

"Hey! Who you think you are?"

One of the boys, a black as tall as she, tried to pull the ball from her hands. She spun round, knocking him to the concrete, and shot again, banking the ball off the backboard neatly into the net. She grabbed it once more.

Now all the boys were after her. She began to run across the playground laughing and clutching the ball to her chest. She could hear the boys screaming behind her, but she was too fast for them. She ran in and out of hopscotch games and right through jump rope, all the way back to the basketball post where she shot again, missing wildly in her glee.

The boys did not watch for the rebound. They leaped upon her. She was on her back, scratching and kicking for all she was worth. They were yelping like hurt puppies.

"Hey! Hey! What's going on here?"

Miss Harris towered above them. The fighting evaporated under her glare. She marched all seven of them to the principal's office. Gilly noted with satisfaction a long red line down the tall boy's cheek. She'd actually drawn blood in the fracas. The boys looked a lot worse than she felt. Six to one — pretty good odds even for the great Gilly Hopkins.

Mr Evans lectured the boys about fighting on the playground and then sent them back to their homerooms. He kept Gilly longer.

"Gilly." He said her name as though it were a whole sentence by itself. Then he just sat back in his chair, his fingertips pressed together, and looked at her.

She smoothed her hair and waited, staring him in the eye. People hated that — you staring them down as though they were the ones who had been bad. They didn't know how to deal with it. Sure enough. The principal looked away first.

"Would you like to sit down?"

She jerked her head No.

He coughed. "I would rather for us to be friends."

Gilly smirked.

"We're not going to have fighting on the playground." He looked directly at her. "Or anywhere else around here. I think you need to understand that, Gilly."

She tilted her head sassily and kept her eyes right on his.

"You're at a new school now. You have a chance to — uh — make a new start. If you want to."

So Hollywood Gardens had warned him, eh? Well, so what? The people here would have learned soon enough.

Gilly would have made sure of that.

She smiled what she knew to be her most menacing smile.

"If there's anyway I can help you — if you just feel like talking to somebody . . ."

Not one of those understanding adults. Deliver me! She smiled so hard it stretched the muscles around her eyes. "I'm OK," she said. "I don't need any help."

"If you don't want help, there's no way I can make you accept it. But, Gilly" — he leaned forward in his chair and spoke very slowly and softly — "you're not going to be permitted to hurt other people."

She snuffled loudly. Cute. Very cute.

He leaned back; she thought she heard him sigh. "Not if I have anything to do with it."

Gilly wiped her nose on the back of her hand. She saw the principal half reach for his box of tissues and then pull his hand back.

"You may go back to your class now." She turned to go. "I hope you'll give yourself — and us — a chance, Gilly."

She ignored the remark. Nice, she thought, climbing the dark stairs. Only a half day and already the principal was yo-yoing. Give her a week, boy. A week and she'd have the whole cussed place in an uproar. But this afternoon, she'd cool it a little. Let them worry. Then tomorrow or maybe even the next day, *Wham*. She felt her old powers returning. She was no longer tired.

Written by Katherine Paterson
Illustrated by Jane Tanner

ONE OF THE PACK?

Thirteen-year-old Miyax has run away from home because her father and stepmother had arranged for her to marry a boy she did not like. For an Eskimo girl, already yearning to know more of the gussacks' (or white people's) way of life, an arranged marriage was too much.

Miyax hastily packed a rucksack with some food, a few essentials and a cooking pot, then set out to walk to the coast. She intended catching a ship to San Francisco, to visit her pen friend Amy — the one who calls her Julie.

But Miyax has lost her way. Her food is all gone and she is weak with fear and hunger. With no way of catching food for herself, she must either die or display a different kind of courage needed to survive in the Alaskan wilderness — to trust other living things.

Her father Kapugen had told her once that wolves will sometimes feed others than their own kind, if they realise there is a need. For the past two days she has been watching the pack constantly. Their leader is a large black wolf whom she has named Amaroq, but she still cannot understand the signals he makes; nor, it seems, does he yet understand her . . .

A dull pain seized her stomach. She pulled blades of grass from their sheaths and ate the sweet ends. They were not very satisfying, so she picked a handful of caribou moss, a lichen. If the deer could survive in winter on this food, why not she? She munched, decided the plant might taste better if cooked, and went to the pond for water.

As she dipped her pot in, she thought about Amaroq. Why had he bared his teeth at her? Because she was young and he knew she couldn't hurt him? No, she said to herself, it was because he was speaking to her! He had told her to lie down. She had even understood and obeyed him. He had talked to her not with his voice, but with his ears, eyes, and lips; and he had even commended her with a wag of his tail.

She dropped her pot, scrambled up the frost heave and stretched out on her stomach.

"Amaroq," she called softly, "I understand what you said. Can you understand me? I'm hungry — very, very hungry. Please bring me some meat."

The great wolf did not look her way and she began to doubt her reasoning. After all, flattened ears and a tail-wag were scarcely a conversation. She dropped her fore-head against the lichens and rethought what had gone between them.

"Then why did I lie down?" she asked, lifting her head and looking at Amaroq. "Why did I?" she called to the yawning wolves. Not one turned her way.

Amaroq got to his feet, and as he slowly arose he seemed to fill the sky and blot out the sun. He was enormous. He could swallow her without even chewing.

"But he won't," she reminded herself. "Wolves do not eat people. That's gussak talk. Kapugen said wolves are gentle brothers."

The black puppy was looking at her and wagging his tail. Hopefully, Miyax held out a pleading hand to him. His tail wagged harder. The mother rushed to him and stood above him sternly. When he licked her cheek apologetically, she pulled back her lips from her fine white teeth. They flashed as she smiled and forgave her cub.

"But don't let it happen again," said Miyax sarcastically, mimicking her own elders. The mother walked towards Amaroq.

"I should call you Martha after my stepmother," Miyax whispered. "But you're much too beautiful. I shall call you Silver instead."

Silver moved in a halo of light, for the sun sparkled on the guard hairs that grew out over the dense under-fur and she seemed to glow.

The reprimanded pup snapped at a crane fly and shook himself. Bits of lichen and grass spun off his fur. He reeled unsteadily, took a wider stance, and looked down at his sleeping sister. With a yap he jumped on her and rolled her to her feet. She whined. He barked and picked up a bone. When he was sure she was watching, he ran down the slope with it. The sister tagged after him. He stopped and she grabbed the bone, too. She pulled; he pulled; then he pulled and she yanked.

Miyax could not help laughing. The puppies played with bones like Eskimo children played with leather ropes.

"I understand *that*," she said to the pups. "That's tug-o-war. Now how do you say, 'I'm hungry'?"

Amaroq was pacing restlessly along the crest of the frost heave as if something were about to happen. His eyes shot to Silver, then to the grey wolf Miyax had named Nails. These glances seemed to be a summons, for Silver and Nails glided to him, spanked the ground with their forepaws and bit him gently under the chin. He wagged his tail furiously and took Silver's slender nose in his mouth. She crouched before him, licked his cheek and lovingly bit his lower jaw. Amaroq's tail flashed high as her mouthing charged him with vitality. He nosed her affectionately. Unlike the fox who met his mate only in the breeding season, Amaroq lived with his mate all year.

Next, Nails took Amaroq's jaw in his mouth and the leader bit the top of his nose. A third adult, a small male, came slinking up. He got down on his belly before Amaroq, rolled trembling to his back, and wriggled.

"Hello, Jello," Miyax whispered, for he reminded her of the quivering gussak dessert.

She had seen the wolves mouth Amaroq's chin twice before and so she concluded that it was a ceremony, a sort of "Hail to the Chief". He must indeed be their leader, for he was clearly the wealthy wolf; that is, wealthy as she had known the meaning of the word on Nunivak Island. There the old Eskimo hunters she had known in her childhood thought the riches of life were intelligence, fearlessness, and love. A man with these gifts was rich and was a great spirit who was admired in the same way that the gussaks admired a man with money and goods.

The three adults paid tribute to Amaroq until he was almost smothered with love; then he bayed a wild note that sounded like the wind on the frozen sea. With that the others sat around him, the puppies scattered between them. Jello hunched forward and Silver shot a fierce glance at him. Intimidated, Jello pulled his ears together and back. He drew himself down until he looked smaller than ever.

Amaroq wailed again, stretching his neck until his head was high above the others. They gazed at him affectionately and it was plain to see that he was their great spirit, a royal leader who held his group together with love and wisdom.

Any fear Miyax had of the wolves was dispelled by their affection for each other. They were friendly animals and so devoted to Amaroq that she needed only to be accepted by him to be accepted by all. She even knew how to achieve this — bite him under the chin. But how was she going to do that?

She studied the pups, hoping they had a simpler way of expressing their love for him. The black puppy approached the leader, sat, then lay down and wagged his tail vigorously. He gazed up at Amaroq in pure adoration, and the royal eyes softened.

Well, that's what I'm doing! Miyax thought. She called to Amaroq. "I'm lying down gazing at you, too, but you don't look at *me* that way!"

When all the puppies were wagging his praises, Amaroq yipped, hit a high note, and crooned. As his voice rose and fell, the other adults sang out and the puppies yipped and bounced.

The song ended abruptly. Amaroq arose and trotted swiftly down the slope. Nails followed, and behind him ran Silver, then Jello. But Jello did not run far. Silver turned and looked him straight in the eye. She pressed her ears forward aggressively and lifted her tail. With that, Jello went back to the puppies and the three sped away like dark birds.

Miyax hunched forward on her elbows, the better to see and learn. She now knew how to be a good puppy, pay tribute to the leader, and even to be a leader by biting others on the top of the nose. She also knew how to tell Jello to baby-sit. If only she had big ears and a tail, she could lecture and talk to them all.

Flapping her hands on her head for ears, she flattened her fingers to make friends, pulled them together and back to express fear, and shot them forward to display her aggression and dominance. Then she folded her arms and studied the puppies again.

The black one greeted Jello by tackling his feet. Another jumped on his tail, and before he could discipline either, all five were upon him. He rolled and tumbled with them for almost an hour; then he ran down the slope, turned and stopped. The pursuing pups ploughed into him, tumbled, fell, and lay still. During a minute of surprised recovery there was no action. Then the black pup flashed his tail like a semaphore signal and they all jumped on Jello again.

Miyax rolled over and laughed aloud. "That's funny. They're really like kids."

When she looked back, Jello's tongue was hanging from his mouth and his sides were heaving. Four of the puppies had collapsed at his feet and were asleep. Jello flopped down, too, but the black pup still looked around. He was not the least bit tired. Miyax watched him, for there was something special about him.

He ran to the top of the den and barked. The smallest pup, whom Miyax called Sister, lifted her head, saw her favourite brother in action and, struggling to her feet, followed him devotedly. While they romped, Jello took the opportunity to rest behind a clump of sedge, a moisture-loving plant of the tundra. But hardly was he settled before a pup tracked him to his hideout and pounced on him. Jello narrowed his eyes, pressed his ears forward, and showed his teeth.

"I know what you're saying," she called to him. "You're saying, 'lie down'." The puppy lay down, and Miyax got on all fours and looked for the nearest pup to speak to. It was Sister.

"Ummmm," she whined, and when Sister turned around she narrowed her eyes and showed her white teeth. Obediently, Sister lay down.

"I'm talking wolf! I'm talking wolf!" Miyax clapped, and tossing her head like a pup, crawled in a happy circle. As she was coming back she saw all five puppies sitting in a row watching her, their heads cocked in curiosity. Boldly the black pup came towards her, his fat backside swinging as he trotted to the bottom of her frost heave, and barked.

"You are *very* fearless and *very* smart," she said. "Now I know why you are special. You are wealthy and the leader of the puppies. There is no doubt what you'll grow up to be. So I shall name you after my father Kapugen, and I shall call you Kapu for short."

Kapu wrinkled his brow and turned an ear to tune in more acutely on her voice.

"You don't understand, do you?"

Hardly had she spoken than his tail went up, his mouth opened slightly, and he fairly grinned.

"Ee-lie!" she gasped. "You do understand. And that scares me." She perched on her heels. Jello whined an undulating note and Kapu turned back to the den.

Miyax imitated the call to come home. Kapu looked back over his shoulder in surprise. She giggled. He wagged his tail and jumped on Jello.

She clapped her hands and settled down to watch this language of jumps and tumbles, elated that she was at last breaking the wolf code. After a long time she decided they were not talking but roughhousing, and so she started home. Later she changed her mind. Roughhousing was very important to wolves. It occupied almost the entire night for the pups.

*   *   *

"Ee-lie, okay," she said. "I'll learn to roughhouse. Maybe then you'll accept me and feed me." She pranced, jumped, and whimpered; she growled, snarled, and rolled. But nobody came to roughhouse.

Sliding back to her camp, she heard the grass swish and looked up to see Amaroq and his hunters sweep around her frost heave and stop about five feet away. She could smell the sweet scent of their fur.

The hairs on her neck rose and her eyes widened. Amaroq s ears went forward aggressively and she remembered that wide eyes meant fear to him. It was not good to show him she was afraid. Animals attacked the fearful. She tried to narrow them, but remembered that was not right either. Narrowed eyes were mean. In desperation she recalled that Kapu had moved forward when challenged. She pranced right up to Amaroq. Her heart beat furiously as she grunt-whined the sound of the puppy begging adoringly for attention. Then she got down on her belly and gazed at him with fondness.

The great wolf backed up and avoided her eyes. She had said something wrong! Perhaps even offended him. Some slight gesture that meant nothing to her had apparently meant something to the wolf. His ears shot forward angrily and it seemed all was lost. She wanted to get up and run, but she gathered her courage and pranced closer to him. Swiftly she patted him under the chin.

The signal went off. It sped through his body and triggered emotions of love. Amaroq's ears flattened and his tail wagged in friendship. He could not react in any other way to the chin pat, for the roots of this signal lay deep in wolf history. It was inherited from generations and generations of leaders before him. As his eyes softened, the sweet odour of ambrosia arose from the gland on the top of his tail and she was drenched lightly in wolf scent. Miyax was one of the pack.

Written by Jean Craighead George
Illustrated by Allan Jane

110

WORDS TO WOLF

Glossary

agouti *(p.28)*
a hare-like burrowing animal

calcined *(p.42)*
solidified burnt ash

capers *(p.45)*
quick jumping movements

compensated *(p.62)*
made up for it

corroboree *(p.49)*
Aboriginal dance festival

dasheen *(p.27)*
also known as taro; a broad-leaved plant with starchy edible roots

doleful *(p.78)*
dismal

ere *(p.78)*
before

fatalism *(p.62)*
acceptance that certain things will happen and cannot be changed

ferocity *(p.62)*
fierceness

fracas *(p.101)*
noisy quarrel

frost heave *(p.102)*
a higher piece of ground lifted due to freezing below the surface

gouting *(p.64)*
gushing

gullible *(p.73)*
easily fooled

herald *(p.75)*
messenger

imbecile *(p.94)*
stupid person

immortal *(p.75)*
lasting for ever

lamenting *(p.75)*
mourning, grieving

mia-mias *(p.42)*
Aboriginal temporary bush shelters

molasses *(p.27)*
thick syrup, treacle

Glossary continues on page 112

Where would an astronaut leave a space ship?

At a parking meteor.

obscenity *(p.94)*
rude word

optimistic *(p.52)*
looking on the bright side

salvo of shots *(p.53)*
shots fired at the same time

sandspit *(p.82)*
narrow ridge of sand stretching out to sea

sapodillas *(p.27)*
fruit, also called sapodilla plum

sassily *(p.101)*
cheekily, impudently

shard *(p.57)*
fragment

wharf *(p.81)*
landing place where boats may tie up to load or unload